HOW DO YOU EXPECT ME TO BE YOUR *WIFE* WHEN I'M SO BUSY BEING YOUR MOTHER!?

R.I. LINDNER

WIN WIN PUBLICATIONS
LAS VEGAS

Win Win Publications
6108 Iron Kettle Street
Las Vegas, Nevada 89130
First printing 1996.

ISBN 0-9658644-0-5

LCCN 97-090595

TO RE-ORDER
PLEASE CALL
(702) 440-9559

DEDICATION

This book is dedicated to my son Bobby. His extraordinary love and wisdom as a young boy made it all possible. My fortune in having him in my life can not be expressed in words. I love you very much. Thanks Monk.

ACKNOWLEDGMENTS

Appreciation falls short of expressing my gratitude to all those that contributed to making my dream come true. There are literally hundreds of people I've met over the years that have contributed to the writing of this book and to my own growth. I am indebted to the following people for their encouragement, friendship and unconditional caring. I would like to thank my mother, not only for her love, but for the courage and wisdom that showed me the beauty in the simple things of life. She taught me to explore my creative skills that made looking beyond what my eyes could see and my emotions could feel, passionate and alive. My dad taught me the "never give up spirit" that it took to overcome all the obstacles along the way. My son Bobby showed and gave me love and words of wisdom that no other person in my life ever gave. Thank you Bobby and Karen for going to the circus that one afternoon and giving birth to the title. Toni you gave me the confidence in my skills in story telling. Charlotte, I am forever indebted to you. You defined friendship that all men once in their lifetime should have the fortune of possessing. You made this book possible with your encouragement, but more important, you brought the first group of women to me to share their stories. Therese, you were and are still beyond a friend. You laughed at my stories and gave me support that made my dream a reality. I will not attempt to make a roll call of all the women I had the fortune of listening to and learning from. There are 223 women I personally interviewed. There are parties I attended that I listened actively and passively to that, as the inividual parent, I heard the most private stories to be told. The checkout lines at the markets revealed some of the best stories in the book.

There were parks I took my son to. Wherever I went I listened carefully to what all the moms had to say. I listened to the talk shows on radio and TV, read article after article in the magazines and newspapers from around the country, attended dozens of support groups and frequented many more places that women were found on a daily basis. I had the fortune of listening to their every day realities. Pam, you helped financially at a time I needed to get the book through important stages. I have to especially thank the many readers, male and female, that made this book a reality. Loretta Tefft and Jason Tefft, Rachel Johnson, Barbara Crisman, Brad Smith, Scott Easely and Stephanie Ford helped create the cartoons. Wendy Bohannon contributed as a reader, listener, confidante and designer of the cover. Day after day she'd be there to compare, test, argue, share, listen and then help create the cover and book we have today. Patricia Lamb used her artistry with words to bring life to many stories and emotions. She proved how valuable an editor is to a writer. Without her artistry there wouldn't be a book today. Kimberly Adams not only proved how lucky I am to have her as a friend, but she edited my stories to make sure everything was consistent with being a story for women. Kate McHale-Lewis took the book and put the finishing touches on the pages. She helped make it read so that you, the reader, feel like you're looking through the eyes of the characters. Miki Lekic and Howard DeAlvarado, your artistry to put it all together in book form, turned my words, pictures and life into a book, thanks. I have a very special thanks to all the ladies in my life, all my girlfriends that taught me to be more aware. They taught me how to listen and hear, not just listen. I want to thank, in so many ways, my business partner for the book and very special friend, Ron Portaro. He helped turn the obstacles into a dream come true and gave me encouragement to see that the dream was not a dream, but a reality. To everyone, I am forever grateful and probably will never be able to ever pay you back. I hope I can give out, like you gave to. Thank you.

FOREWARD

We all have a desire to be loved. Some get their love by taking care of others; some get their love by feeling like they're being taken care of. We're so filled with expectations that we often don't have a mind of our own. We have expectations from parents, friends, teachers, employers, society, children and the list goes on. What a mess. We start relationships expecting one thing, and then we either change our mind and say "it wasn't what I was expecting" or "it was what we we're expecting, but it wasn't what we really wanted". Sounds confusing doesn't it?

When my son was about six years old, I took him to the circus with a female friend and her son. I noticed during the show that a lot of children were resting their heads on their mother's shoulders. I was surprised. I told my friend how nice it was to see how affectionate the kids were, especially the boys. When the lights were turned on for intermission, I was shocked to see that many of the people I thought were children, turned out to be adult men. When I pointed it out to my friend, she didn't look surprised. In fact she said to me "I'm not surprised. Just yesterday my girlfriend was talking about her husband and said, 'How does he expect me to be his wife when I'm so busy being his mother?'" Being a single parent, her comment really made me think a lot about expectations in male and female relationships. It really wasn't the first time I had heard the statement, but for some reason, it really bothered me that day.

When I went home, I remembered how many women thought they had to take care of my son and myself, even though I was doing everything just fine. It was assumed by many ladies, that I needed help. What was going on that so many women thought that way about men?

I asked myself, "Why was it so important in relationships, that with all the complaining, it was still going on and what would happen if it stopped?"

I decided to begin listening to what women of all ages and cultural backgrounds had to say. I knew I wanted to be loved like everyone else, but I didn't want to have someone in my life that thought she had to do everything for me. After years of interviewing, I decided to put the stories the women had to tell in a book. It didn't matter where I went, the stories repeated themselves over and over again. I learned a lot beside the obvious, that men and women are different. I learned a lot about expectations. I learned a lot about communication and perception.

I wanted very much for women to know they're not alone and for men to know they really are consistently doing the same things everywhere I went. I'm not blaming anyone. But with awareness, maybe change can occur. If men were like little boys, women had to consistently do things that perpetuated it. And if men were acting like little boys, the men had to be consistently doing things that perpetuated it too. Both must be getting something from their actions. Otherwise, it would have stopped a long time ago. If I wanted it to stop for me, I had to listen carefully. What I learned is told in this book.

There are stories you'll laugh about; there are stories you'll cry about; while others may even anger you. The stories are so real, you may wish you could just shake some of the ladies and say, "Stop talking about it already; get on with your lives." Some readers may feel offended by what some stories have to say and some may deny their own behaviors with the men in their lives.

These are your stories. If I had heard them only once, I would have questioned their validity, but I heard the same stories over and over again, from all parts of the country, from all different cultures and from all different ages—only the names and faces changed.

I hope you'll enjoy the book and maybe stop and think of what men and women expect of themselves, to be loved versus what they think they really want. When they admit the difference, then they will know how to improve their relationships. If anything, I hope we all stop and listen to the ones we love and really hear them. I also hope we all stop and listen to what we are telling ourselves and be sure it's the same as what the people in our lives perceive.

CHAPTER 1

I wonder what would happen if I fell down the stairs and broke my leg? Maybe my back too. Nah, that would get to them, but the pain would be greater than my satisfaction. I have it! Maybe today I'll try a coma. No, comas are good, but they only arouse sympathy. Comas are for soap operas anyway. No, something more potent would be in order at this stage of frustration. I have it! Suicide. That's it. Suicide. I'll have to be careful about how I commit suicide because, knowing my husband, he'd stand around waiting for me to make his dinner before he'd let me go off and die. Oh and who'd clean up the mess? I wouldn't really do something stupid like that. It's just that over the past few weeks, I've fantasized about every possible way of causing guilt in my family. I don't mean just a little guilt. I mean real, deep, lasting guilt. The kind of guilt that brings me a glowing satisfaction for all the years of neglect and emotional deprivation I've gone through.

Fantasy can really be fun. I don't ask a lot, just a little recognition, that's all. I once read an article back in my college days, around 1969, on the subject of "woman" or "female" (and by a man—oh, what a surprise), which had been well received. His thesis was that God didn't create woman from Adam's rib to give him a partner; rather, He created woman to punish man. He believed that if God was only concerned with   procreation, He would have given man his very own vagina, so that he could screw himself, at least literally instead of figuratively, like he already knew how to do. He even wrote that menstrual cycles had three purposes, all of them designed to punish man.

First, this writer said that, "The real reason a woman had the kind of period she had, was to endlessly frustrate men (never mind that she had to endure pain and the image of her body swelling). God didn't have to give woman hormonal changes every month—you know, that twilight zone you step into when man finds himself running for his life from someone who only slightly, physically resembles his perfect woman. No, it was done so woman would be moody, irrational and just a royal pain in the ass, to punish man. Then, the final reason was to prepare man for his woman to become pregnant, which, if you're a husband, you have to know that her throwing up every morning, her absolute irrationality, her getting fat, and her loss of sex drive were all rigged by God just to punish men." That was only a small sample of what he had to say.

As you can imagine, the Sixties woman was up in arms. Looking back, I kind of admire that guy. At least he had the guts to put his stupidity in writing. Most men just practice it, and then they have the audacity to praise women on Mothers' Day with flowers and presents, beaming in adoration as if their purpose in life was to treat her like a queen (the next day, of course, life goes on like normal). So here I sit, feeling tired and sorry for myself, for being the best at what I was trained and expected to be, a modern day woman. I was given my first perfect child on my wedding day; that's right . . . my husband. Growing up didn't prepare me for the reality part of marriage, only the fantasy of having the perfect family. In fact, when Steve and I got married and the minister asked me to say the words "I do," I didn't realize I'd be the only one doing. Two years after the perfect wedding, I had my first perfect male baby. I didn't realize then just how perfect my son Bobby was. First, I had the perfect pregnancy. I threw up perfectly and I had a perfect thirty-seven hour labor. But what came out was a perfect 9 lb. 4 oz. baby boy. He grew up to be even more perfect. He learned to drop his clothes on the floor perfectly. He watches TV with the remote control perfectly. He is perfectly helpless around the house. He will become another perfect husband. My sister then got pregnant, so wouldn't you know, I got pregnant again. After all, I couldn't let her out do me. My daughter Suzie emerged into the world after only a two hour labor. She scares me though. She didn't come out a baby. She came out a miniature woman. When she played with her first doll house, she knew exactly how to take care of all the perfect male dolls, arranging them in the recliners aimed at the television (of course, all the female dolls were always in the kitchen).

With all that perfection in my life, you're probably wondering about me. My problem is that I'm expected to be perfect too. How did I get to be so imperfectly perfect? Ah, well, that's another story . . .

"YOU MAY THINK YOU'RE A SUPERBOY, BUT I'M NOT YOUR SUPERMOM."

"UNDERSTAND!!!"

CHAPTER 2

Thirty eight years, four months, three weeks and six days ago, it all began. My mother has been telling this story for so many years that I'm sure if I ever get reborn into another body, the impact of that story will be so deeply ingrained in my soul, it will be as physically real as a leg or an arm. My parents were one of those post-World War II couples who would produce those wonderful Baby Boomers and Yuppies, and though they didn't realize it then, they would also produce the very first MUT. I'll get to MUTs later.

Mom and Dad were also one of the courageous couples to wagon-train it out to the farm fields of Long Island and begin tract housing. The fathers would "tract station-wagon", driving hours every day in tract car pools to the City, while their pregnant wives (who looked like "tract pregnancies", each identical to the next) came in and out of each other's new tract houses, helping to decorate and prepare a life for their "tract families".

Our town was not far from where the Godfather was supposed to be making offers that people couldn't refuse. Oh well, there are lots of offers in life that people don't seem to be able to refuse. Mom, one-quarter Italian, one-quarter Jewish and one-half whatever she wanted at the moment, sat with her best friend Florence, both of them looking about as pregnant as you can be, both of them stuffing their faces with everything that Florence told her they were supposed to eat. After all, they couldn't starve their babies. And besides, they had the right to eat now for all the years they had deprived themselves of good things to eat because they had to stay fashionably skinny to get those perfect husbands they ended up with. Now they had permission, in fact, doctor's orders, to eat to their hearts content. Sitting in the next room from my mom and Florence was the origin of my problems. Don't get me wrong; I love my Dad very much, but my problems began even while I was in the womb. Like all other dads, mine had to have a boy. Now this was nothing unusual, but he drove my mother crazy, not just with the typical things that husbands do, but with things that went a little too far.

One night during a ladies card party, someone told my Mom that she'd have a boy because she was carrying low. Obviously, my Dad was very happy to hear this. So the rest of the evening that's all Dad could talk about. But that wasn't enough for him. He called his Mom the next day to ask her opinion. Still doesn't sound that unusual, does it? Be patient. Dad was just getting started.

In the middle of the following night, Dad started talking to Mom's belly. Men do this all the time to their pregnant wives, but not at three in the morning, and especially not like my Dad. He used this peculiar feminine voice and said things like, "What color do you think we should paint the bathroom?" Then he put his mouth inches from her belly and began using that peculiar feminine voice again, "Where do you want to go shopping tomorrow? What was that wonderful recipe for the chocolate chip cookies?" After each question, he'd feel Mom's belly and then give a big sigh of relief. Mom told me that she didn't have the heart to interrupt him and anyway, if she had, she would have missed all he fun. So she pretended to be sleeping soundly. That still wasn't enough to satisfy Dad. He stared at her for a few minutes to make sure she was still asleep, which didn't make much sense. And then, like a typical man, he started announcing a baseball game that would have awakened anybody, "And it's a long ball. It's going, going . . . gone! And the Yankees have done it. They win!" God must have sent down a sign just for Dad, because he started cheering. Mom couldn't pretend she was asleep any longer. "What the hell are you doing?" she asked, trying to keep back her laughter, knowing very well what he'd been doing, but she didn't want to miss the fun of hearing him explain it.

"It's a boy!" he cheered. "He moved. He kicked when I talked baseball to him, and not when I talked all that female junk, like cooking and shopping." He sat there with a silly, little boy's smile. Then, with sudden realization turning to reddening embarrassment, he rolled over and pretended to be asleep.

Mom had nothing to say. She couldn't let his great expectations down. She covered her face with the blanket, not knowing then that this episode was just the beginning. That should have been enough for him, right? Wrong! Dad was convinced that he needed more proof. So without asking Mom, he invited some women from where he worked over to the house to serve up a buffet of wives tales, anything to get his little boy. Why Mom put up with all this silliness, I don't know. My Dad even kept score as if it was a ball game: Girls team 3, Boys team 12. (Oh, what a surprise.) What Dad didn't realize was that I kicked because he got all excited. The louder he cheered, the more I kicked. Any normal father would have been satisfied, but not my Dad. Even though the opinion that I was a boy was unanimous, Dad felt that something had to be wrong; it was just too perfect. Perhaps, he thought people were biased because they knew him, and they knew he desperately wanted a boy.

All this was bad enough, but then Dad crossed the line from acceptable eccentricity to complete absurdity. He put an ad in the classifieds without telling Mom. It read: "Wanted: Specialists in the area of predicting babies' sex while still in the womb. Experience required." One afternoon, Mom had already had her belly painted, watches and chains dangled over her, chanting and singing from a guy dancing solemnly around her, and whipped cream slathered on her stomach (it would melt for a girl, and stay firm for at least thirty seconds for a boy). The list went on. Then the doorbell rang yet again. When Mom opened it, there stood a Gypsy, an American Indian, and some guy wearing a fancy turban. They all had the classifieds page with the weird ad in it, and they asked her if she was the lady seeking methods to determine the sex of her unborn child. After the shock at seeing these three strangers, Mom slammed the door in their faces, screamed, then barged into the den where my father more or less lived, watching baseball games on the tiny TV set (small compared to the giant TV set he's married to today). She stomped over to the TV, switched off the game, and started yelling at him.

"That's it! I won't do this ever again. I don't know why I've put up with it this long. You want a boy? Well, forget about it, Buster. Just for what you put me through the last few weeks, we're going to have a girl. I don't care if it's already a boy. I'm going to change it and you can remember all through the rest of your life that it was your fault!" Which had about as much logic in it as Dad's fruitless search. But Mom turned out to be right. I was born a girl as a punishment to my Dad. Thanks Mom and Dad, both of you. To this day he thinks I'm really a boy who just came out looking like a girl. I don't want you to think my Dad didn't love me, but I have to live with the fact that I was second choice, out of two choices, great for the old ego. My Dad did everything he could to teach me what he would have taught me if I really had been a boy. Mom worked just as hard as she could to make my life different from hers. She just wasn't sure what that was supposed to be. Sounds confusing. It was. So I became a feminist. That was as confusing to me as growing up a by-product of Mom and Dad.

A feminist was a woman who wanted the equal right to have and do what a man has and does, and still be a woman. When I grew up, I met women with the same ideas. We attended a lot of rallies and sit-ins, passed out leaflets and sent letters and telegrams to Congressmen. I'm not sure that any of us really knew what we wanted. Until recently, I even had a separate walk-in closet for all my personality changes.

The other day, while putting on my makeup, I took a good look at myself in the mirror. Before I finished painting on the face I needed to be a female professional and cover up the Supermom look I was so proud of here at home and was about to leave behind, I realized that somebody had come up with the label "Supermom" as if to put a medal on women who did it all. It was a lot like being given a plaque for all our efforts. That label unfortunately stuck and it made those women who didn't feel they lived up to that image feel perfectly guilty for not being able to do it all. Well, I'm no Supermom. Sure, I try to do it all. Or rather, I'm expected to do it all. I tried to keep up that image for years. I even believed what everyone was saying because it made me feel special and needed. Not anymore. I'm not perfect, nor do I even want to be. Perfection would only give my husband an excuse not to do anything at all around the house instead of the little he does do.

So, I became a MUT. Doesn't sound too appealing, does it? It stands for Modern Urban Triumph. I was raised by my family at home and by the feminists out in the world to be perfect. I was raised to believe that I could do it all. When I couldn't anymore, I didn't dare tell anyone. I couldn't allow myself to be a failure and let everyone down. So the more I believed them, the guiltier I felt. For my own salvation, I became a MUT, what society expected of me. I did the shopping, washing, cooking, nursing, doctoring, listening and all the rest of the "-ings". I'm not saying that my husband never did anything, but he had to be asked first and that's not the same as actually doing it.

MUTdom beckoned to me. I believe that Supermom is a label created by a man to take advantage of the feminist movement. Supermoms are perfect. They're not allowed to feel guilty over not being perfect in every way. After all, how could anyone perfect feel guilty? In the end, every woman who tried to be a Supermom locked herself into her own jail and swallowed the key. So I became a MUT. They're not perfect; they're merely great. Are you asking what's the difference? Here it is. MUTs' are allowed to complain and I do my best to live up to being a MUT, at least that part of it. If we didn't complain we'd continue for the rest of our lives feeling guilty for not doing everything for the "perfect" little boys in our lives. So I complain. Does it help? I guess it depends on how much I complain.

"DON'T BE AFRAID. I PROMISE THERE'S NO SUPERMOM IN THIS HOUSE!"

CHAPTER 3

Although the term Supermom was coined back in the heady Sixties, the concept came from the days of dowry offerings by fathers who were either financially in bad straits or extremely cheap and who wanted to catch a rich, eligible, prospective husband for their daughters. A true Supermom was worth a king's ransom. Many parents have tried to raise a true Supermom, but it's not that easy. You can't just teach Supermomism from a book. True Supermoms are unfair freaks of nature that emerge from the womb already perfect.

Even the birth process is void of any pain for her mom. The Supermom baby sleeps through the night without a sound from the start, leaves perfectly shaped poops in her diaper, and the diaper barely even smells. The Supermom baby is destined from the start to grow up perfectly and become every other woman's nightmare. If you are ever cursed in life and unfortunate enough to have one of these rare creatures as your friend, do whatever you can to drive her from your life.

If you think the expectations placed on you by your family are bad, just try the torture of having a Supermom in your neighborhood and constantly being compared to a pseudo-goddess. I am one of those women to whom you would have been justified in sending sympathy cards. My well-intentioned attempts at being the perfect Mom to my husband and children were gone forever because of her.

I have a neighbor and friend who is, unfortunately, one of them. I first met Babs, the infamous Supermom in my life, the day she moved in across the street. What a perfect name for a Supermom. Same source as Barbie.

Before she finished unpacking, she showed up on my doorstep with the welcome wagon. That's right, she brought a welcome wagon to me. It sounds perfectly neighborly, doesn't it? Babs eloquently made me feel really welcome to a community that I had lived in for two years, while she had only moved in that day. Only a Supermom could pull that one off. You had to see what she brought over, brownies and all different kinds of cookies on a perfectly arranged platter (real china, not plastic, of course). All this had been done while she was still unpacking. She couldn't have had the time to bake; I didn't have the time to bake, even on my day off, never mind on moving day. Everything was perfectly baked. The cookies were all the same size and annoyingly moist and chewy. Besides tasting wonderful, what was most depressing was that I lost weight after eating them. The excitement of a two pound weight loss was crushed by the realization that it could be attributed to eating cookies and brownies baked by a Supermom. It did make sense, in a perverse way, of course. I don't know about your baking experiences, but I only have to look at my own recipes to gain weight. It just wasn't fair. Why did she have to choose me as her neighbor? To this day, I don't know what I did to deserve the punishment.

I still didn't know what I was getting into until I went to her house while she was unpacking. Have you ever seen a home being moved into by a Supermom? It was spotless. Her floors were not only clean, they were shiny and newly waxed. Floors don't shine when you move into a new home. I should have known I was in trouble when I saw that her furniture was in place already, as if she had twitched her nose, and Voila!—the house was decorated.

Even with that lesson, I still didn't completely understand. But over the next few weeks I learned what a true Supermom does compared to the mere impersonator, the Modern Urban Triumph. We spent every day together for about a month and, without fail, her family's clothes were always clean. Everything was folded and neatly put away. "How does she do it?", I asked myself constantly.

The meals were always prepared precisely on time, set on a perfectly arranged table with fresh flowers daily. Everyone was seated together; she never had to beg to get her family to come for dinner. This was odd, because my kids played with her kids, and every evening around six, I could be heard screaming at the top of my lungs to get them to come to the table from the Jungle Gym in the back yard, or from inside the headphones of their stereos, or from the infamous video game.

Even when she first woke up her hair was always fixed, just like the soap opera actresses. She never had bad breath, as if she had been born with a mouthwash patch that gave off tiny sprays of mouthwash as needed. She probably sweated deodorant, because when I snooped one day in her medicine cabinet, I couldn't find any. Yet she never had any body odor, even after exercising. I often wonder if she ever suffered from gas problems. Nah, she was probably perfectly cool, calm, and collected, a state of mind that automatically converted her gas to liquid, so that she couldn't have gas even if she wanted to.

Maybe I'm exaggerating a little, but knowing my husband and his friends, they'd love to invite her to move in just to make their wives feel guilty for not being like her.

And then, of course, in the great American female tradition, we both tried to lose weight. She really didn't need to, but she said humbly how hard she worked at keeping her weight down. Yeah, sure. She didn't realize that Supermoms don't ever have to worry about things like that. They just have to be humble and rub our noses in it. We decided one day to buy a Richard Simmons aerobics tape. She stood in place, moving her head up and down to the music. I danced and danced and sweated like a pig. She lost weight, and what she lost, I gained. The perfect balance. I wanted to puke, but then I'd be accused of being the only bulimic who ever gained weight.

It gets worse. I always wondered why Babs's house never had ants, roaches or garbage odors; everything was perfect. I'm convinced that bugs never moved into her home out of fear that they would have to be too perfect to be allowed to stay. Bugs knew better than to go to her home. They'd die of boredom. What would they do? What would they live on? Why should they bother? Now, take my home and trust me, they did. Even though I slaved to wash, clean, scrub, mop and sanitize, they apparently found my home very exciting. My kids kept them challenged. They probably even had their bug relatives come to my house on their vacations because of all the activities my family had planned for them. Now, if you were a bug, who would you rather live with?

She was so perfect that you know she had to have a perfect dog too. What do Supermoms dogs do? They never leave little messes on the neighbors lawns, therefore, they must have little baggies that catch their little poops. Let's look at my dog. He probably watches her dog and poops where her dog doesn't (sympathy poop). Can you guess what kind of reputation I have with the neighbors? She was also involved in every committee at her children's school and every community volunteer program. She did all this and more, and still worked at a full time job. I never heard her family complain. Her children were always polite. I'm getting nauseous just writing about them.

She's never tired and never has bags under her eyes.

16

Knowing her as I do, I'll bet you that she even smiles during PMS. Well, I'm not a Supermom. I'm a Modern Urban Triumph, and I'm tired. I'm tired of doing everything. I'm tired of everything being my responsibility. I'm tired of being expected to be there for everyone regardless of how I feel or what I need. I'm tired of being Mom to my husband. I'm just plain tired of being expected to be and do all this. And most of all I'm tired of being compared to Babs. My Mom once told me that little girls grow up to be mothers, while little boys grow up to be little boys. When I was a little girl, I didn't know what she meant. I think, because I idolized my Dad, nothing my mom said about men and women made any sense to me, or I didn't want to hear it.

Unfortunately, it took getting married and three children of my own for me to learn. Now that I'm knee-deep in marital and family MUT bliss, I don't know how to change my life. Sometimes I feel completely helpless. And other times, I feel like I'm doing everything I'm expected to do. Sounds normal, doesn't it? My husband blames it on the hormones; my kids listen to their father. So who do I get to blame it on, my mother?

I swear that today is going to be different. Today something in the air told me that it was time. Today I will cross over into another dimension. Today will be the day I will lose my logical reasoning and just live by what I feel. Today will be my day. The only thing that matters is me. I feel no more need to be responsible. No guilt. No fear of failure. I will take no more discounting from anyone, especially my husband. The glorious feeling of not having to be everything for everyone temporarily places me in the territory typically reserved for men. By the end of the day, I got so good at expecting others to do for me that I thought I had actually grown a penis, even if it were only for a day. No need for a big one, of course—just big enough to understand what it was like to have some woman do everything for me, not because she wanted to, but because she was obviously, expected to. It was an interesting emotion I was experiencing. I felt like a kid again, but with all the power of an adult.

Today started out like every other day. Normally, I wake up at 5:30, wash my face and put on makeup before I exercise. My husband can't understand why I put on makeup before exercising. I put it on because it makes me feel good. When he goes jogging, he doesn't shower or shave, he doesn't wear any deodorant, nothing. He complains that people are unfriendly when he jogs in the morning, but says they're different when he jogs in the afternoon. He can't understand that people can probably smell him half a mile away. Now where was I? Oh yeah. I slipped into my spandex and turned to see whether he was watching. When we first got married, he used to wake up and watch me dress. It was kind of exciting, watching his hormones dance around like they did. But something happened somewhere along the way. His staring became ogling. Now he doesn't turn to look unless he expects a quickie. No seduction. No sensuality. It's so frustrating. I work very hard to stay in shape so that I look good for him (and of course me too) and all he thinks is that as long as he gets hard, he's fulfilled his end of the bargain as a lover.

I'm not sure why today was different from any other day. Maybe it was something my husband did. Actually, knowing my husband, it probably was something he didn't do? It doesn't matter. I had enough of everything and everybody. I was angry. No, anger was not the right word. I was frustrated and tired. I was behind schedule today, especially after making everyones beds, cleaning the bathrooms, folding the clothes, finally showering, rushing to put on my makeup, putting on another of my boring dress-for-success suits, planning who needs what, when, how fast, and at what time. Of course I was going to be late for work again. Do you think my family cared? I doubt it. My kids (including Steve) were probably only concerned with why their breakfast was not on the table yet.

I could just picture my husband tapping his fork impatiently on the side of the plate, and the kids getting annoyingly noisy. Like the perfect wife and mother I guess I am, I took a deep breath and proceeded to go down to take care of my family. "They have to eat properly, no matter how angry I am," I thought, using MUT logic. I slowly went down the stairs, trying to compose myself back into MUT cheerdom, but instead, feeling my sense of frustration again.

When I got to the bottom of the stairs, I paused for a moment. I could see through to the breakfast room, but they didn't see me. I took stock of the four of them, my four children (my husband included), waiting for my services. Finally they noticed me, one by one. I looked deliberately at each of them in a way that would show them that something was definitely wrong. I didn't say a word, because I didn't want any of them to know what they'd done wrong (not hard, because there was always something they'd done wrong). I strolled slowly to the breakfast room arch, leaned against it, put my hand dramatically to my forehead. After all, if I wasn't saying anything, there had to be some way of letting my husband (the leader of the four) know that I had a splitting headache already and that it was their fault. However, they just sat there and blankly looked at me, obviously not getting it. So I looked at my husband and said calmly, "Honey, I've got a splitting headache. I'm angry and I'm tired, but let me ask you a question. How do you expect me to be your wife when I'm so busy being your mother? Can you think about that simple thing for me?" Not expecting an answer, I slowly moved away into the living room, where I couldn't see them anymore. I stood there, wondering what he was thinking. I doubt that he knew what I was talking about. I pictured him in the other room, holding up one finger, it not being the thumbs up sign. That's the way he fights back. It's always the finger and that annoying look on his face, unless it's his other response: "Oh God, she's got PMS again." My husband was amazing; he knew I wasn't having my period, and I'm too young for menopause. Therefore, it had to be something he had done and he could never admit that. As a result, I knew he would be wielding his favorite weapon as if that finger had some magical power.

WHEN I GROW UP LIKE DADDY, CAN I HAVE A WIFE TAKE CARE OF ME TOO?

CHAPTER 4

I call my street Plastic Lane. When I leave every morning at exactly the same time to go to work, everyone on the block seems to leave their home exactly seconds after I do. Each and every one of us perversely dependent upon the corporate time table, seemingly choreographed by the pressures of having to work to keep the privilege of living on Plastic Lane with all the rest of us. I have this recurring fantasy. One day I will intentionally leave half an hour later, just to see what will happen. There they will be, waiting for me to come out. I can just hear them muttering, "How dare she do this to us? Why is it so hard for her to leave on time? She has a responsibility to all of us!"

I'm not sure what frustrates me more. My feeling responsible for everyone or other people's expectation that everything is my responsibility. I watch these TV shows with the mothers who have to do everything for their families. Their children talk about how their wonderful mothers sacrificed themselves for their families. Does this mother look as if she regrets having spent her life doing all this stuff? Not at all. She sits there crying tears of joy, looking proud as punch at having played a domestic Mother Teresa. The audience then cries with her and the legacy of the martyred woman gets perpetuated. Then all the women in the audience try to be like the woman on the show spending her one and only life attempting the impossible. No wonder why so many men expect the women in their lives to be that way, too. And we parents complain about too much violence on TV for our kids. What about the psychological violence we suffer from the shows we love to watch? You know what it's like? It's like that guy in Europe a long time ago that I read about—Greece, maybe? He did something wrong, and for his punishment, he had to spend his whole life pushing a big boulder up to the top of a steep mountain, and when he got there, some joker at the top just gave it a shove and down it rolled again. This poor fellow had to go down and start all over again. So what we do is punish ourselves with our own roles we continually play on tv and the real world, perpetuating the expectations that go along with being born a girl.

For instance, women are forced to think they should be skinny like the perfect models in all the magazines, TV shows and movies. So we kill ourselves trying to fulfill the expectations of everyone around us, and worst of all, try to be like those women. Why? To be attractive to the very men we later have to take care of; those men who have become our extra child. Who cares about looking great for just another pre-teen boy? I'm tired of being expected to be something that may not be possible. You see the perfect bodies on TV and in the magazines. You know that these are probably the result of self-destructive eating habits. Well, being the perfect woman is also probably the result of self-destructive behaviors.

Not anymore! Today I feel like being nasty. I feel like shaking everybody up, maybe even leaving a few mouths hanging open. I'm not going to tell everyone I've had enough. I'll show them. PMS won't be the excuse. I don't even have PMS. When Joe Johnson, our favorite neighbor and my husband's golfing partner, asks me how I am, I won't be the sweet and wonderful person I normally am. I'm going to look him in his bland blue eyes, smile innocently and say, "Tired, drained, emotionally used," and then the nasties will pour out of my mouth leaving his mouth hanging in shock. Oh boy, will the nasties fly. Then my face will return back to the sweet lady I always portray and I'll say, "How's your day?"

After leaving him with his jaw hanging open, probably thinking the same thing my husband thought, I could then concentrate on Mrs. Johnson, who can always be found watering her flowers. Then, expecting my typical sweet response, sweet, boring Mrs. Johnson will say brightly, "Off to work this fine morning? How are the children? And Steve, of course? How is he today?" I'll look her in the eye, give her back her sweet smile and say anything and everything that will leave her in complete shock. Then, as quickly as my face changed to the nasties, my sweet old smile will return and mechanically say, "How's your husband?"

Whew, the nasties will fly. Maybe I'll do it all day. Maybe that will be enough to let everyone know something has to change. Maybe they won't have any idea they're doing anything wrong, and all I'll accomplish is they'll think Jenny has flipped out. I don't care. I'll feel better. Well, here goes. There's Joe coming out of his house. A few more steps. I'm really going to do it. Yes indeed. Are you ready Joe? "Good morning, Jenny. How are you today?"

"Fine, thanks. And you?" I can't believe I didn't do it. Maybe instead of calling me a Modern Urban Triumph, I should call myself Gutless Wonder. Well here come the rest of the neighbors, right on schedule. My smile gets pasted on automatically. A smile, by the way, that I think comes with my makeup kit, something I learned to put on to make me look socially acceptable. I guess it's time to fulfill my responsibility to my neighbors. After all, I wouldn't want to ruin their day. I could just hear them all showing up at work saying, "It's Jenny's fault." And everyone will understand. The cosmic law of the neighborhood will return to normal and all will be forgiven, at least for them.

Do you have any idea how many people's lives I might ruin by changing so suddenly? I don't think I could be that selfish. I mean, think of everybody at their jobs being infected with my irresponsibility and the people they'd infect. People at the supermarket, people in restaurants, even people sitting in traffic jams, not to mention their families and friends. I don't think I'm ready yet for that much responsibility. Well, here are the rest of the neighbors.

"Hi, Jenny. How are you?" they'd ask. "Just fine. Ha, ha, ha, ha!" (a laugh put on like my makeup).

"Your kids are getting so big." I feel better now. Everyone's day will be safe. So I didn't do it. I know I have to. Someday. I have to.

I promise. Really. Well, maybe I do. I don't care if you don't believe me, but I really will do it. You'll see.

Shut up Jenny! You talk too much.

CHAPTER 5

Maybe by this time, you think I'm just another neurotic mess. Well, I wasn't always the way I am today. I grew up in an upper-middle class neighborhood on Long Island. And, regardless of my Dad's obsession with the son he's still convinced was stolen from him, I was pretty happy. In high school, I was a cheerleader. I dated the football team quarterback, a couple of the basketball players, a wrestler, and . . . hmmm, I guess I dated a lot of jocks. I was a sorority sister, voted prettiest smile for the yearbook. I experimented a little with sex, like all my friends back in the Sixties. Even so, I wanted to be unique, to have my own identity, but I had to wear the same styles that all the girls wore. How else could I remain popular?

My dreams were typical: have a career, marry a rich, handsome husband, raise two and-a-half perfect children. So what choices did I mull over? Should I become a career woman? Or a clone of my Mom? The women's movement solved that problem for me. Since we were striving for equality to men, why not do both? After all, why not prove to men that we're better than them, that we can do both? Now, if you think about that a second and put yourself in a man's shoes, would you argue with that way of thinking?

If we wanted true equality, here's the way we should have done it: go to school, start a career, put money in the bank. Then when it was time to have a baby, why actually go through nine months of nauseating, fattening pregnancy? I read an article about a surrogate mom who gave birth to her own grand-daughter. My own Mom loved being pregnant. Why not let her do it for me? Well, if we wanted children, why not let our moms have the babies for us? That way we could sit around after work, watch TV, find someone else to cook dinner for us, have someone raise the kids, except for playtime with them. Working steadily at a good job through all these stages would bring in the necessary money. We could leave the sports to the husbands while we went shopping. Now that's equality. Don't get me wrong. I loved taking care of my babies, the nurturing and bonding was very special. There's no way I would have ever given it up. I guess I'm just tired. Lately, I've been "Whoa is me-ing" a lot.

How many of you have wished that your husband could have gotten pregnant instead of you? Which one of you got up every morning looking forward to throwing up your toenails? Which one of you loved getting fat and waddling around off-balance, having sore breasts and Preparation H as your best friend. And then, going through labor! Pushing eight pounds of flesh and blood through an opening two sizes too small, just like the jeans my husband wants me to wear. Is there a one of you who wouldn't give all that to your husband to experience?

I don't want you to misunderstand, I loved the feeling of my babies inside of me. When I first felt my baby move, there was no way to explain the feeling of love I had. The bonding I experienced was worth all the discomfort. What I'm trying to say is I wish my husband could have gone through what I went through, just once. I could have used a little empathy for the parts of pregnancy I could have done without; the parts of pregnancy that if he went through it just one time, maybe I would have received more compassion, more help. If he could have been pregnant for a week, that's all I think he needed. No, we didn't get equality. We did everything our moms did, and we had a career (with unequal pay, I should add). Now, how much did the men change? I know there are a few men out there who are changing a little, or at least trying to change, but compare that to all the women who go on doing it all. Which one of you really knew what she was getting into before she got married and had children? Which one of you dreamed about going to work all day long, only to come home to have to clean the house, pick up after a man, cook for him, wash the dishes for him? Do, do, do, do, do.

Don't get me wrong! I love all my children, including my husband Steve. My point is, that if we wanted equality, we didn't really get it and I don't know if I'd ever really want it. Do I sound contradictory and mixed-up here? Well, I love my children and I love my husband, and at this point in my life, I can't see how it's ever going to be possible to be the "unique" me I dreamt about as a young girl and the woman with all these responsibilities that I turned into. I guess I'm just feeling a little overwhelmed right now. I keep thinking about the years I spent in college with all the rallies against the war, rallies for equality, sometimes rallies for no particular reason. It was an emotional time, a frivolous time, a time of dreams. It was a time when I didn't have to . . . I just didn't have to. My life then was just the opposite of what it is today. I'm always too busy to dare to stop. I have too many people depending on me to stop. I've forgotten what it feels like to do something that I'm not supposed to do. I've forgotten the excitement of doing anything that's a little dangerous . . . or maybe just frivolous. All day long at the office I work on problems. I come home and work on more problems. I go to meetings resolving more problems. I get together with the ladies and talk about still more problems. Sure, we laugh about them, but we still spend what seems like all of our time on problems. And our problems are not exactly who's going to win the election this year. I've now reached the point that when I go out to relax, I can't seem to have any fun unless there's some problem to be solved. I don't even know if the fun I have is really very much fun.

One day I was thinking about this as I mopped the kitchen floor. I yelled to Suzie and Bobby to come downstairs. I looked at them very seriously and told them to go out and have fun because when they grew up, they wouldn't have the time to do it anymore. Oh, I saw that little look pass between them that said plain as day, "Mom's flipping out again." But at least I had warned them of what was to come. Not my fault if they choose to ignore the warning. Funny, isn't it? We teach our children to grow up and act mature because one day they'll have to be responsible adults and have to go out partying and act like a kid to have fun. Logical, right? Where's my boulder to push up that hill?

Why do women accept the role of mother so eagerly? And why do most women feel so guilty if they're not there for everyone? Who says it's automatically our responsibility? Imagine when we were children, we were told that one day we'd be grown women, meet a handsome man, fall in love, think he was the only one for us, get married and have the glorious opportunity to follow him around the house picking up everything that he left on the floor. We'd cook, clean and compete with sports for his affections. We'd have to do that and a lot more, "til death do us part". Would you marry knowing all this ahead of time? Or maybe you wouldn't believe it and would blindly charge down the altar anyhow. Your husband was going to be different. You could make your perfect little life go the way you wanted it to go. Just like my kids apparently think that there's a lifetime of fun ahead of them.

Generation after generation, we raise little boys to be little boys and little girls to be mothers. Steve says he can't help the way he is; it's in his genes. He told me with a touch of smugness in his tone that "back in prehistoric days, men had to go out and hunt for the family and protect them. Women were required to stay home in the cave and take care of everything else. When the man came home from the hunt, the woman had to nurture him so he'd be rested up for tomorrow's hunt. Because men don't have to go out hunting anymore, God provided them with sports and television. You see, God wanted it this way."

I couldn't believe my ears. He wasn't kidding. But he's got it wrong anyhow. Men go to jobs now instead of the hunt. But the women, most of them anyway, go to jobs too. Who's going to nurture me when I get home to the cave every night, huh? What women keep forgetting is that little boys are trained by both women and men to be taken care of. We're just as guilty for their education as the men are. But the men put such gunk into their son's heads. Let me give you an example. The other day I was finishing up in the kitchen (why do so many of my best and worst moments seem to have come in the kitchen?) and was listening to the conversation my husband and son were having while they were playing basketball outside. My husband was educating my son in the fine art of making a woman happy. "Just remember," Steve said, "whenever you do something to help your Mom or your future wife, don't do it completely." He paused to take another shot. My son ran to get the ball. I was transfixed at the window taking all this in, without being seen. "Sure," Steve continued, "she'll get angry and frustrated, but in reality, she'll be happy. You have to understand Bobby, that women need something to do, and as much as you can give them to complain about, the happier they are. It's in their genes. Never forget that. Don't listen to what they say. Watch what they do." "But why?" asked my son with a disarming innocence. "Got me?" my husband answered. "I just know that women are happiest when they're doing things around the house. But, in their joy, they spend a lot of effort to convince us that they hate it. If they hated it so much, why would they all do it? Why? Because, as I said before, they can't help it. It just is a fact of life." Having delivered these nuggets of wisdom, silence came over this domestic philosopher as he shot a few more baskets, Bobby standing respectfully on the sidelines. He went on. "You see, Bobby, the more we leave for them to do the more love we're really showing them. But don't leave it all for them to do. Always show them that you're trying, but just can't do it right. Then they take over and feel important. I think this was one of the gifts that God intended to give us when he made 'Woman.'"

"But Dad, how do you know?" asked my curious son. "I mean, what if you really did help?" He was obviously confused at the adult male's logic. "Let me give you an example, son. When you were a baby, I stayed home once to take care of you while your Mom went shopping. She asked me to do some chores around the house while she was gone. I did such a good job that there was nothing left for her to do. When she came home, she acted pleased that I did such a good job. But she was really confused. When she thought I wasn't paying any attention, she walked around the house looking for things that were not done. She was unhappily happy." Steve looked at Bobby closely, to see if the boy was following this unbeatable male logic. "So I learned something. Now I leave something undone. She complains. She knows I tried as hard as I could, for a man. She's happy. I'm happy. And that's the secret to a great marriage, except for great sex, of course." They both laughed at that, and went off on a new tack with their male bonding.

A conspiracy. A male conspiracy. But he was only partly right. I do walk around looking for things not done correctly. He was only talking about the things I ask him to do, though. What he forgets are the things to be done that I don't ask for, so if I don't go around checking, who will? Not my husband.

IF DONNA REED HAD MY FAMILY THE SHOW
WOULD HAVE BEEN CANCELED.

CHAPTER 6

I didn't become the teacher that my parents wanted me to become, but I did become a career woman. I took an ordinary nine to five job after college and made it a career position. What bothers me though, is that I'm not sure why I originally did it. Was it because I really wanted a career? Or was it simply that all my girl friends wanted careers and I didn't want to be like my Mom and just stay home and take care of my husband and wait for the babies to come.

Maybe I should have listened to Mom and Dad. Those summer vacations would have been nice. On second thought, I'm having a tough enough time as it is with one bunch of children to take care of at home. I don't know if I could have handled another set at school. Mostly I love my job. Besides, we need the paycheck. Not that my job at home with my family doesn't have its rewards. I mean, I love my family very much, as I keep saying, but I think they would prefer having Donna Reed there for them. I feel that they want a Mom who does everything perfectly and doesn't need anything in return. I think they want me to be in love with taking care of them, that it's all I look forward to each day. For years I tried to be Donna Reed for my family, but I just couldn't figure out how to wake up every morning with my hair already done and my makeup fresh. I'll bet you that Babs is related somehow to Donna Reed. She did everything so easily. She always had a smile beaming out of the TV screen, even when there was nothing to smile at. I'll bet you the Stepford Wives slept with the Donna Reed Bible of Motherhood next to them in case something came up they didn't know how to deal with.

The more I try to do at work and at home, the more guilt I feel at the thought that I'm not doing enough. Why is it that men never feel guilty for watching too much sports and not spending enough time with their kids and wife? Why is it that I'm proud of myself for being good at my job but feel guilty that my kids are being deprived? When things get really hectic, I become a fast food Mom. I even keep a bunch of menus in my car, and depending on what I pick up first, that's what I fast-cook that night. Some of my girl friends came up with the idea of home-cooking co-ops. One night a week, each one of us would cook for everybody. This good idea worked out fine, until some of us started either going out and buying from a restaurant what we were supposed to be cooking or leaving it up to the husbands to do it. That was funny because there were times when we couldn't tell the other ladies what was cooked even with the food in front of us. We ate UFO's (unidentifiable food offerings). We eventually went back to feeling guilty. At least that was more appropriate for a true MUT. One time I was so disgusted with everything and everybody that I made a vow to myself, no more guilt feelings anymore. Then I felt guilty that I was becoming more like my husband and couldn't feel guilty. That was the secret, to feel guilty for not feeling guilty. Now I'm tired and I want everyone to know it. Maybe it'll make me feel better. Maybe we'll share feeling guilty. Hey, that was a joke! You were supposed to laugh.

**NO! NO! NO! NO!
NOOOOO!
THAT FELT GREAT!**

CHAPTER 7

The past three months I've been staying in my office later and later. But I'm not sure whether I'm staying because I have legitimate work to do or whether I'm just avoiding going home to the work there. So tonight, as I've done every day since this all started, I sit at my desk, talking to myself, wondering what I'm still doing here, knowing in my heart that I'm avoiding the domestic routine that lies ahead of me. Should I phone Michelle? Oh, I forgot to tell you that I have a good female friend. She's a little weird, sort of a left-over hippie, but I still share a lot of all this with her and she shares with me. But, as we all know, you can't moan and groan all the time. You won't have many friends left.

So I talk to myself. "Come on, Jenny, pick yourself up. Go home. You don't really want to stay here at work, do you?

You know your family needs you. You know you're using work as an excuse to avoid your children. Besides, you don't really want to hit the worst of the traffic and sit in a two hour bumper-to-bumper, do you? Jenny! Go home! You can't just sit here anymore! You have to do something, one way or the other. Now! Get up!"

I'm in trouble, aren't I? I mean, I know talking to myself is supposed to be normal but I'm enjoying these conversations too much. The problem is I can talk to myself about anything I want, as often as I want (well, as often as I can get solitude). I don't ever get looks from myself that say, "What the hell are you talking about?" the way I do when I try to talk to Steve. At least I get intelligent answers to my questions when I talk to myself. And even when I lose an argument with myself, I don't get all bent out of shape. There's never any fear about hurting someone's fragile ego. I never go to bed angry with myself for what I did or didn't say to myself. And anyway, even in bed I can sort it all out and say it right.

I think that's what's really bothering me. I'm enjoying the conversations and at the same time feeling guilty that I'm doing something wrong at home that's making me resort to talking to myself. And that's assuming that I even get the occasional privilege of a conversation at home. When the old TV set is on, nothing else exists for Steve, nothing else of course except food and sex. And the children, well, they're not much better. Now, maybe, you can understand why I avoid going home. You know what's really sad? It sounds like a normal American family, doesn't it? They seem happy enough. I should be happy. So what's the problem? The truth is, I don't want to live this normal middle class family life anymore. I don't want to go on feeling like just another fixture or appliance. I can see the real estate ads now, "This house comes with all appliances, including mother-of-the-family, built-in and working either from batteries or plug her into the wall outlets anywhere in the house." Yeah, Jenny, the super frig/stove/vacuum/freezer, etc. I want to go on the TV show, Lifestyles of the Struggling and Infamous. I want to be different. I'm tired of feeling like there's something wrong with me. If things don't change soon, the woman of the future will have to have miniature TV sets built into her breasts for her husband ever to pay attention to her. Maybe there are other ways of getting everyone to fight over who needs and loves good old Mom more. True, we still won't have any time for ourselves but at least that way the husbands would pay some attention to us. Then again, we'd still probably be a fixture in the house. But they'd have to treat us as someone special.

I wonder if I could get a surgeon to experiment on me? I could go down in history as the perfect wife of the future. I could see myself standing in line in the supermarket and reading in the tabloids about the surgery that was done on me: "The most popular Mom in the world resorts to surgical implants for true and lasting happiness." So here I sit at work, avoiding my family and using work as the excuse that I can't go home. And, in a perverse way, enjoying it.

I can see my family, my adoring children (Steve included), all at home waiting for Mom. After all, it's getting close to dinner time. So they wait. Honestly, it's not their waiting that bothers me; it's that they expect me always to do it for them. No, it's not really the expectation that bothers me. I mean it does, but it's the fact that I go ahead and do it anyway that's really disturbing. So I sit at work talking to myself, surrounded by the janitors, avoiding my family, instead of doing something about it. Maybe if I avoid facing them, they'll all grow up and go away and then I can be who I really want to be. Can I stay here at work for ten years and just order in Chinese and pizza?

I know the answer is simple. All I have to do is "Just say no," and that's not to drugs, Nancy. Or maybe it is a drug. After all, it is an addiction, isn't it? In many ways it's the same as what young people go through with drugs and peer expectations. What's the difference? Both are pleasurable in the beginning. Both are continued without any real benefits to oneself. Both are expected. Both are voluntary. Both are ended apparently only when rock bottom is reached. Both are never cured, but controlled. Both create guilt. Both sound so simple to stop, but they're not. I always give in. It's not that easy for me. I try, but if I say no and leave the responsibility for my husband to do everything, my children are in trouble. Actually, my husband is the one who's in real trouble. I know I'm a Dr. Frankenstein and I've created a monster, but I can't just say, "No". I'm afraid of child endangerment. I know that's not fair to say about all men, but you haven't met Steve yet. I have to give them time. Maybe all I have to do is wait till the kids grow up. What could be so hard about that? No! Stop it, Jenny! I know that one day I'm going to have to say "No". So I've been practicing saying "No", just in case I decide to do it without warning. I could go on strike. One of the ladies in the office read a cartoon about that. Maybe not yet. Maybe if I just learn to say no more often. I have to practice so I can get so good at it that when the day comes, and the words come spewing out of my mouth, I'll be so smooth and proficient that I won't even be tempted to back down.

I've been rehearsing saying "No" for months now. After what I went through this morning, I might just begin tonight. They deserve it. But I must be prepared. Instead of the drive home through smog and traffic being the usual exhausting and frustrating chore, I've actually been having fun. You have to picture me getting in my car, starting the engine. Then I begin to sing. I can start with any song. The actual song doesn't matter. Usually I go along with whatever is on the radio. But I have my own lyrics, thank you very much. All I do is to start singing the word "No", in a soft voice. It sounds something like this: "nooooooooooooooooooooooo!   nooooooooooooooo NnnoOnononononononoNOOOOONNNNONONONOO?
N   o
Nooooooooooooooooooooooooooooooooooooooooooo! No!
No! NO? n O   OOOOO! nononono no
NOOOOOOOO   nnnnnnnNNNoN   ooooooOOOOOO
NNNNNNNNNNNnnnnnnnNNnnnnNOooooooNnonononno
No!   NONOnnnnnooonnonononono
N   N   N   O   O   O
N   O

                    NONO   O
nnnoOOnnNOOOOOOOONnoooo   no

nonoooooooooooooooooooooooooooooooooonnnnnnnnnnnnnn nnnnnnnnnnnnno! I practice saying "No" to everyone. It's great. Try it some time. I was even thinking about making a tape just to hear me saying "No" every way there is to say it. I have a few self-help tapes; is there anyone who doesn't? How To Stop Smoking. How To Find Self Esteem. So maybe I should try to market one: A Thousand Ways of Saying No. Anyhow, I look at it as my own kind of self-help. But, "Oh, golly gee," as Gomer used to say, has it really helped me at this point? Picture me sitting in my car. The windows are rolled down. I'm singing, screaming, whispering, whining, and everything in between with any kind of "No" in it. It works with everything: Christmas carols, rock, country western, even opera. Everything works! Would it work with dialogue? Like, "To be or not to Be?" No, no. NO nono. But I guarantee you, it's cathartic. Here,

T   R   Y   I   T.
NOnononoNNONONONnNNONONONONONONONO
NONONONONONONONONONONONONONnono
nononononoooooooooooooooooooooooooonnnnnnnn
o o o o o ! N O ! N O ! N O N o N o N

NoNONONONONONO!!!!!!!!!!!!!!NNNNNNNNNnnnnnnn
nNNNNNNNNNoooooooNooNo! God, but it feels good. I especially love it when people look over at me in the car and try to figure out what station I'm listening to, one they can't get. And they sure can't recognize the song I'm singing. They probably wonder how I can be happy in traffic. Try it!
N N N N N N N N N N N N N N N N N N N N N N N N o !
NNNNNNNNNNNNNNNNNNNNNNNNNNNNNNNNNN
NNNN

O O O O O O O O O O O O O O O O O O O O O O O O O O n !
OOOOOOOOOOOOOOOOOOOOOOOOOOOOOOOOOO

OOOO   JUST ONE LAST TIME: I 'm f o c u s i n g

NNNOOOOOOOOOOOOOOOOOOOOOOOOOOOOOOOO
OOOOOOOOOOOOOOOOOOOOOOOOOOOOOOOOOO!
IT'S GREAT! I'm ready.

Wait! ONE MORE TIME!
NONONONONONONONOnonononononononoNONONON
OnnnnnnnnnnnnnnnnnnOOOOOOOOOO

OOOOOOOOOOOOOOOOOOOOOOOOOOOOOOOOOO
OOOOOOOOOOOOOOOoOOoOoOoOoOoOoOoOoOo
No! Yes.   Oops! I mean, No.

                    I'm ready!
                    You go girl!

BUT MOM, IF YOU ONLY KNEW HOW HARD IT WAS BEING A MAN, YOU'D UNDERSTAND WHY I CAN'T CLEAN MY ROOM ANYMORE.

CHAPTER 8

Supermarkets—sometimes I think they are part of the male conspiracy against working women. They know we always end up in them on the way home from work and they know we have to come home eventually. Men know they can wait us out. Easy to do with a couch, remote control, tv set and a ball game. Heaven to my husband. I have to stop at John's, the closest supermarket to my home. Why I go there, I don't know. The check-out lines are ridiculous. The only consolation is that there are a lot of other people as ridiculous as I am, all standing in line, leafing through The National Enquirer or Star, which they put back on the stands when their turn comes to unload the cart. Even the Express Line is usually so long at 5:30 that the word Express should be removed. It's as long as the other lines but everyone keeps standing in it because it says Express. The regular lines usually have about six to eight heaped shopping carts. We all wait and wait. I perform this idiocy Monday through Friday. Well, maybe not every day, but at least three times a week. Strange how, just out of habit, people are willing to put up with these lines. I used to talk to the people in line, but I'm tired of talking about how long the lines are and howhigh the prices are.

I know, yes I do, you don't have to say it—if I went earlier, once a week, I could avoid all this aggravation. Then again, if my husband would help, I wouldn't have to deal with this problem. He says all I have to do is write out a list for him and he'd be more than happy to help. To begin with, why do I have to write a list? What's wrong with him? He can look in the fridge and cupboards. He can write. He can drive. He can push a cart and stand in line. Who said it was my responsibility in the first place? All that macho stuff says that men historically went out and hunted to get the food. So why not hunt in John's instead of in the forest primeval?

And then he makes it sound like he's going to do me a favor. Why can't it be something he does every day or every Monday and Friday? Then he could ask me to do him a favor occasionally by doing his shopping.

I hate having to write a list, so I put up with the lines. Anyway, I always find things to pick up that I wouldn't have put on the list, and Steve would never have noticed them or thought about buying them.

Don't get me wrong; there are times he helps. I have written the occasional list for him but that's usually over the weekend. I guess that's just another part of the old routine. Would you agree with me that "routine" is at the root of all boredom? Yet we try to structure our lives to be efficient, so we get caught up in routines. Have you ever had FUN with a routine? What does that tell you? So I head to the supermarket, once again, because I'm a good wife and mother, and I can hardly let them all starve to death or get malnutrition from living on chicken noodle soup or fastburgers. There are times, late in the afternoon after the traffic builds up and the smog blankets everything, when it is at its thickest and most poisonous, that the sky is at its loveliest. An iridescent red-orange glow fills the western sky, softening the edges of the city, mellowing me out like a really good glass of wine. For the short time this phenomenon takes place, the whole world seems to stand still in the illusion of God's worldly creation, just too beautiful to be real. My life seems to be like that illusion in the sky. Those who look at it see beauty; those who know better smell and see the poisons. Yet there are days when even I get caught up in its beauty. I'm like that smog-created beauty. I too don't know what it is to be real, but I can create interesting illusions. After all, look how many people I've fooled just like the sunsets.

The line at the supermarket wasn't too bad today for a change. They opened up checkstands usually left closed. I think they open extra stands to fool the public sometimes, to make them think shopping at 5:30 isn't going to be so bad at their market. It's amazing how many of us fall for it. Today there was only one lady in front of me and she had just a few items in her cart. She fiddled with her purse until she finally pulled out a few coupons plus a ten dollar bill. She looked to be in her late seventies. I watched her while she was fumbling for her money. I saw that half her groceries was cat food. I think her groceries would have been very different if she weren't so poor.

I recently read an article in a magazine called "Pet Gossip" that said many senior citizens would rather feed their animals than themselves. Either way, it was sad. If the food was for her pet, then she was going without food for herself. If the food was for herself, then she had to eat cat food. I couldn't help but feel sorry for her. I'm sure the checkout woman noticed all this, but did she really feel sorry for her? Maybe it was embarrassment. Or maybe she sees poor elderly people buying too much cat or dog food all the time. I heard how she greeted her. When she said the usual cheery "Hello!" she didn't even look up at her, never mind smiling. It's sad how we treat our senior citizens. If that had been a young mother with an infant, everyone would be oohing and aahing. I just hope I never get into that place in life. I think it would be better to be dead than to suffer other people's pity. I have a fear of being pitied. I felt embarrassed for her and for myself. I'm sure she has a family somewhere, but they were probably so busy they didn't have time for her. Whether they told her that or not, I'll bet she's the type of sweet old lady who doesn't want to bother anyone. But I'll also bet anything, that when they need her help, she's there without any hesitation. You know what's really sad? When she dies, everyone will probably grieve. They will allremember how wonderful she was. Unfortunately, it'll be too late to tell her, too late for everyone.

Will it stop with her? No. Not as long as women do everything for our families unconditionally. I don't mean that loving men unconditionally is wrong, but living our lives through them unconditionally is.

Easy enough for me to recognize, but I have dug such a big hole for myself that it isn't so easy climbing out of it. So I get angry at them; then I get angry at me for being angry at them and not doing anything about it. Sometimes I actually get ill from the sheer struggle to survive. I know my family cares, but will I one day look like that lady in the grocery line? I mean, here I am, getting their dinner, working all day, doing and thinking for them. I do it because I love them. But is my family's love for me based mostly on what I do for them? Maybe.

HEAVEN IS HAVING TO
PEE AND LOCKING
MYSELF IN MY
BATHROOM WITH
EVERYONE LOCKED OUT.

CHAPTER 9

As the night emerged slowly from the last breaths of daylight, the timed lighting system in my home spun a new illusion of light, preventing the night from swallowing the deceptions I so desperately hung on to. I was just coming over the top of the canyon and could see the lights of our home. I know that hidden behind the illusion of lights are my children, ready to pounce the moment I walk through the front door. To a working mother, the inside of a home filled with hungry children and husband is not anything even a vengeful God would ever have considered creating. At times, coming home from work can be as relaxing as being sentenced to a night in a den of lions.

I'll make you a bet, I'll drive up to my house filled with hungry kids and honk my horn. It won't matter how long I sit there waiting; not a single person will come out to help me. You would think their ravenous appetites would make them gravitate outside and stand in the driveway waiting for me to come home. As I drive around the corner of my street, I notice that every light in my house is on. This is strange because my husband never allows all the lights to remain on at the same time. He's so obsessed with conserving electricity, that he follows me around the house turning off the lights whenever I leave a room. I could be fixing my hair in the bathroom one minute, walk into the bedroom to get something, and find that he has turned the lights off the second I left the bathroom. If all the lights are on, either my husband is not home from work yet, or else he's watching the ball game. Now, if the ball game is on, every light in the house could be burning merrily away and he'd be oblivious. "Well, everyone, Mom's home," I said out loud, as if someone could hear me, as I sit in the car. I begin my homecoming ritual by honking the horn. I then sit patiently waiting exactly three minutes, as if someone, some magical day, might actually come out and help. Just in case they genuinely didn't hear me, I honk the horn again. Do you want a logical reason why I do this? I can't give you one. I mean, I just keep hoping they'll start doing for me like I do for them. I'd be happy if they'd just think of me once, without a reason, other than official ones like Mother's Day or my birthday. Then again, if they ever did think of me first, I probably wouldn't believe it and I'd be wondering what they wanted from me, so I couldn't enjoy their attention. The problem can be solved, of course. All I have to do is to leave everything in the car, go inside, and tell the children to get the groceries. It sounds easy, but it's not. Without fail, whoever I ask will either be on the phone or watching television, and their response is always the same, "Just a minute Mom, let me finish _____". Inevitably, I end up going back out and carrying in the groceries myself. Another reason I don't do it, is because I want them to think of me because they want to, not because they have to. So I sit and wait for what always doesn't happen. I tried to tell my husband one night what I was feeling but all he said was, "Typical!", which is the "typical" length of a "typical" conversation with my husband anyway. "What do you mean, typical?" I asked, knowing that this was all he could say anyway. No matter what a woman did or said, it was always "typical", even when it directly contradicted something else he had noticed the day before that was also "typical". "Only a woman would think like that. Of course we love you. If you want our help, all you have to do is ask." Of course I could ask, but I don't want to have to. It's the asking that annoys me more than the doing of these things. "Honey, when I want you to do something for me, I ask you, don't I? So what's the problem?" He's right; he does ask. He won't do it for himself, so of course he asks. And asks and asks and asks. It's not the same kind of help. I'm always doing; he's always expecting. Why can't the male brain understand this?

So I sit in my car like an idiot again. But don't you see what I'm talking about? Am I the only woman feeling like this? If that were true, I think it would upset me more than actually having to do everything. Please tell me you do understand what I'm going through! Well, I guess it doesn't matter anymore, does it?

Today started out differently and I have a feeling it's going to end differently. By the time I got home, I was fed up with myself again for putting up with everyone's garbage. I honked my horn for the last time and looked at the door to see if someone was going to come out. Before grabbing my groceries, I made sure I put on the same angry face, so that everyone would be sure to see how I felt about them not helping me. I've learned over the years that an angry look and silence get far more results than screaming or banging doors. I also learned over the years that an angry face tells my family that something is wrong, but doesn't tell them who did it or what it is. Of course, they're too selfish to find out on their own, and if I don't tell them, they'll never know, but looking angry and not saying a word satisfies me in a crazy way. Well, the key is in the lock. I pause for one last absurd moment. Listen. Nothing. The door is open. "Mom's home." The attack begins. That announcement came from my son Bobby, probably from the kitchen. I'm not sure which room he lives in more, the kitchen or the den where the big-screen TV is. After all, he thinks we have only three rooms in the house: the bedroom, the den with the TV, and the kitchen. I'm not sure if he learned that from Steve or if it's just in his genes.

How that kid stays so skinny and eats the way he does sickens me. He eats, and I gain weight. It probably all started when I was pregnant with him. I ate and got fat just to keep him healthy. Look at the sacrifice. I had to get fat so he would be healthy. "Maaa, what's for dinner?" I think it's a recording. I don't think there's been a day, no matter where we are or what's going on in the house, Bobby manages to ask, "Maaa, what's for dinner?" No hello, no kiss, just "Maaa, maaa, maaa," over and over again until I answer. But tonight will be different. I'm not going to answer him. And I think I'll use that angry look he knows all too well. I realize that I'm probably fighting against Mother Nature. I'm sure he can't control it, anymore than an animal in heat can. Until satisfied, he'll relentlessly call out the call of the wild: "Maa! Maa! Maa!" "Mother!" That last yell came from upstairs-my daughter Suzie. She came rushing downstairs. "Mother, I've been waiting for you to get home. Can I sleep at Barbara's tonight?" Again, I didn't respond. No "Hi Mom" or "Mother", as she's taken to calling me since reaching the age of nauseating adolescence. No kiss. Nothing. All she had to do was to make one caring gesture and I would have agreed to almost anything she wanted. Still awkwardly holding the groceries, I turned around and walked deliberately into the kitchen, put the bags on the counter, and mechanically thought about preparing their dinner. I would have been happy just to do nothing for a while, but I had my responsibilities to them. You notice I didn't say I had a responsibility to me. I can wait. Why do I do this all the time? Why is it so easy to put my needs last? I know I was taught this kind of behavior from my mom, my dad, my uncles, my aunts, my grandparents, my teachers, my girlfriends, my boyfriends, hhhhh, I guess I could go all day long. But I think you got the picture, right? If I had been taught to jump off a house every day on the way home from work, would I? I'm afraid to think of the answer, especially if it involved my family's needs. It's like that Russian scientist I read about who made his dogs salivate in the lab by ringing a bell every time their food was brought in. Pretty soon they'd salivate, food or no food, whenever a bell was rung. Two kids down, two more to go. Eric, my youngest son, didn't usually raise much of a fuss, so I figured that my husband was next. I was surprised he hadn't come in yet. Normally, as soon as the groceries are put down, he comes into the kitchen to find out what's for dinner. So I guessed that he was watching the ball game. I was experiencing two out of the three uncontrollable obsessions of the typical American male: food and sports. All that was missing was sex, and I know Steve; he probably got an orgasm from the ball game, which would complete the Holy Male Trinity. That obviously explains why Steve was equally obsessed with his remote control as he was with putting his hand down his pants during the ball game. So before I started cooking, I wandered off into the den, and sure enough, there were Steve and my youngest son Eric, mesmerized to the infamous game. What's really amazing was Eric had one hand down his pants, just like his dad. Supposedly, it was the playoffs. That didn't mean much to me, but from the way all the men at work had been talking, it was something of a religious holiday. It must have been, because it appears that almost the entire male population of the country froze into reverent immobility in front of the nearest TV. I walked into our den, and accidentally stood in front of the screen. My husband looked up at me, obviously annoyed. "What the hell are you doing? Can't you see we're watching the game? C'mon, move that butt of yours now." What happened to "What's for dinner?" I said to myself. I guess religious sports holidays outweigh even the call of the dinner table, at least for awhile. So far tonight, I've gone from being a permission slip for my daughter, to a cook for my son Bobby, to an annoyance to my husband. For a moment I felt like the old lady in the supermarket. Not once was anyone concerned about me. Why should they be? I never let them know I had feelings before. I probably created this mess anyway. After all, I took care of everyone so well that there was no reason for anyone to consider that I had needs too. What scares me is, I think they may be right. A little consideration, that's all I'm asking for. Do you know what I mean?

I turned around and started back for the kitchen. I knew that only three urges could disturb the almighty ball game, and they didn't include: sex, hunger, bladder relief and beer. The food, he knew very well, all he had to do was call to the kitchen and I would get it for him. The bathroom, well I'm sure that if I were physically able, he'd ask me to do that for him too. I was almost back in the kitchen when I heard again, "Hey, Hon, what's for dinner?" Obviously a commercial was in progress. Otherwise, there was no way he'd be standing there talking to me. I looked over my shoulder at my husband. I shook my head, not in disbelief, but rather in annoyance at myself that it reached this point, and even worse, that I let it get to me.

"Steve, at this point, I don't even care. All I know is that I've been holding my bladder for a couple of hours now. I've stood in line at the supermarket getting your food. I carried all the bags out of the car, by myself. Now, instead of 'Hi, Mom, how are you?' from the kids, all I got was, "Maa, Maa, Maa." And the only difference between you and the kids is that they don't call me Hon. So if you don't mind, I'm going to the bathroom, and when I'm done, then maybe, if you're lucky, I'll deal with you. Okay?"

I could tell by the look on his face that none of this was getting through to his male brain, and that whatever problems or complaints I had were all my own fault again. I don't think he was capable of understanding what I was saying, let alone what I was feeling. But I didn't care. I had to go so badly that nothing mattered anymore. I think I look forward to going to the bathroom more than anything else lately. It is the only way I get alone time. So I shut the door, put the toilet seat down, another thing I can't get the men in my life to do, sat down, breathed a long sigh of relief, closed my eyes releasing all the day's pressures with it, leaving the rest of the world on the other side of the door.

You don't really believe that lasted, do you? I mean the part about the door keeping everyone out? Don't get me wrong. There are times when it works. Sometimes, when everyone is busy doing their own thing, I shut the door, and even though they are home, I can pretend they're all gone. For a moment in time, I'd be in heaven, in my own world with no interruptions, no demands, just me. Sounds wonderful, doesn't it?

So, whose fault is this one? I guess mine again. I know that when they were little, I always left the door open so they could see me and feel safe. Not them feeling safe. I mean, me feeling they're safe. So I taught them that their mom doesn't deserve the privacy of a closed door, unless of course, Steve's with me. What's interesting is that the same door never seems to get crossed when he's in the bathroom.

Suddenly, my daughter Suzie, stormed into the bathroom. She started spouting off that I never answered her question and that I didn't love her anymore. "Suzie, don't you ever knock?" I asked, knowing she wouldn't answer me, even if she cared. "Mom, it's important. Can I go to Barbara's?" Mechanically, I finished what I came in here to do, pulled up my pants and walked out of the bathroom, making sure I continued to ignore her as I headed towards the kitchen. Suzie followed right behind. "Mother, can I?" Ah, "Mother" again. I knew what was coming next, a change in the tone of voice. When I wouldn't answer her, she used her most effective weapon. She began to whine. She knew that would make me respond. What she didn't know at that point was that I had HAD it. All she had to do was to say something simple, something friendly, like "Hello". Not much. And she could have gone to Barbara's for a week, maybe even a month if I was lucky. Only kidding. But she chose to whine to get her way.

Not tonight. I turned around, looked her right in the eyes, made that famous angry face of mine and lost it completely. It was finally time to put all those months of practice in my car saying "No" to everyone, to work. I just let loose: "No, nonononono nooooo." God, that felt good. It felt better than I thought it would. I think I scared the daylights out of her. She turned and ran upstairs to her room, no doubt to pout and cry about how mean her Mother was.

I turned back and walked to the kitchen, feeling guilty for maybe taking it too far, and at the same time feeling great. I began making the salad, took out the dishes, set the table, and then suddenly stopped.

What am I doing? Let them take care of their own dinner. I turned again, walked into the den, turned the TV off, stood in front of Steve, looked directly into his eyes. Just as he started to say, "What the ..." he realized by my look that I was serious. He didn't dare finish his statement. My eyes said it all. I said to them very calmly, "Steve. Boys. Tonight you are going to take care of your own dinner. I'm going upstairs to be alone. Do you know what that means? If your dad wants to take you out for dinner, he can. If you're lucky, he'll cook for you. I don't care. Just do not disturb me." With that, I slowly walked out of the room, leaving three mouths hanging open in shock. It was great. I felt better already.

I waited outside the den, listening for their reaction. The kids immediately ganged up on Steve. "Dad, where are we going for dinner?" At first I thought Steve was going to get a taste of what I go through every day. But I should have known better. I'll bet you can guess what he said: "We'll decide after the game." There was that game again. If I didn't know any better, I'd say there's something in the male genes that makes them so attached to that TV set and the ball game.

I can just see it now. The guy who invented TV, sitting at his inventor's table, mumbling, "I can't wait to finish! Now men won't have to talk to their wives all night. Now we can have Monday night football, and all day Saturday and Sunday in front of the TV. It will become as holy as going to church. There will be games from morning till night. We'll have sports from around the world, fifty-two weeks a year. It's going to be heaven."

If his wife had known what he was doing to the institution of marriage, she probably would have shot him for the good of womankind.

I walked slowly upstairs, went back into the bathroom, ran myself a hot bubble bath, lit a candle and poured myself a glass of my favorite white wine. I shed my clothes, stepped into the bubbles, laid back, took a slow sip of wine and closed my eyes . . .

MARRIAGE LICENSE DEPARTMENT

WIFE ONLY - $15

MOTHER ONLY - $30

WIFE AND MOTHER - $300

CHAPTER 10

All at once I felt myself rising into the sky. Nothing was
making any sense. I didn't even remember leaving the tub.
It figured. The way things were going for me tonight, I
didn't have a chance of relaxing. I was probably being
punished for abandoning my family and leaving them in the
hands of my husband while I lolled around in the bubble
bath. The question was, where was I? I wasn't sure if I was
sleeping or dreaming. Or, had I drowned in my bubble bath

and was now on my way to Heaven? Whatever was happening, I knew I wasn't afraid. I was convinced that if I had died, I must be going to Heaven. It's my belief that God sends all mothers to Heaven for what they had to put up with on Earth.

I didn't want to open my eyes yet. I was hoping that if I was dreaming, the dream would have a good ending and I would wake up laughing about it. So I waited and waited and waited, but I still couldn't figure out what was going on. Finally, I couldn't wait any longer. I had to know what was happening. I opened my eyes slowly, but quickly shut them again. I was beginning to get a little concerned. Was I really up in the sky? I waited another minute or so, then opened my eyes just long enough to catch a glimpse of billowing clouds all around me, like being in a plane at thirty-thousand feet. I started slapping my face, hoping to shock myself into waking up. I didn't know what else to do. But I couldn't seem to feel the slaps. All right then, I had to be asleep, because nothing else made sense. Okay, I know I'm making something of nothing again. Maybe, if I kept my eyes closed, I would wake up before too long. It suddenly dawned on me, that if I were dreaming, my eyes would already be closed. Now I was really confused. The only way any of this made sense was, that I had to be dreaming that I was dreaming. Even though I didn't know what was going on, I had to admit I was enjoying myself. It didn't matter whether I was dreaming, or was dead. I just wanted to know which one, so I could get on with my current existence. Before I closed my eyes again, I looked around one more time. I was still rising into the clouds. I gave the dream possibility one last chance. I slowly closed my eyes, hoping that everything would go back to normal and I would find myself in the tub again. I counted to ten, as if counting with my eyes closed was going to do the trick.

It's amazing what we resort to when we're at a loss for what would be logical to do. After all, it worked when I was a little girl, so why shouldn't it work now? Besides, I couldn't think of anything else to do. I opened my eyes slowly again, but nothing had changed. Everything was getting stranger by the second. Not only did I continue to rise through the clouds, now someone was blowing a ram's horn that I could hear plainly.

Could it really be possible I was dead? The only reason I could think of why I wasn't dead was that God wouldn't do that to my family. If I died, how would my family take care of themselves? I could just see everyone at my funeral saying, "What a selfish woman, leaving her family all alone to take care of themselves. At least she could have cooked them dinner before dying." If I was dead, it was a nice way of going. Think about it, laying back in a nice warm bath, letting all my worldly problems fade away. No pain, just a smile on my face. Part of me wanted to deny that any of this was really happening to me, so like a child, I put my hands over my eyes. I was convinced that I'd wake up any second and start laughing about this dream, or whatever it was. For some perverse reason though, I was looking forward to going back to being everyone's mom.

What I was going through had to be my punishment for thinking about abandoning everyone tonight. What a sick thought. I couldn't believe I was feeling guilty for taking some private time for myself. It didn't matter how I was treated by my family only five minutes ago. I still felt guilty.

What else could I do but wait until I stopped rising? I could hear some faint talking in the distance. The voices were getting closer and closer. I continued to keep my hands over my eyes knowing that eventually I would have to look at what was happening, but that I wasn't ready to deal with it yet. Although I could hear a conversation going on, I still couldn't make out the words or the individual voices.

It's funny, I was really beginning to enjoy the rising sensation. I don't ever remember feeling so relaxed. I only wished I could stop analyzing what was happening and just enjoy the experience. Too much analysis lately in my life and too little time basking in the moment. Finally, the invisible elevator stopped, or that's how I thought of it by this time anyway. Now I was forced to deal with another situation I didn't want or need. "Jennifer, you think and talk too much, just shut up and enjoy," I said to myself out loud. "Just do it!" "Now I'm really scared, I'm beginning to sound just like my husband." I breathed deeply and slowly took my hands away from my eyes. I suddenly felt a rush through my body, like a wind that could blow through flesh, veins, bones, and for some reason, I knew then that everything was going to be okay. When you hear what happened next, you'll laugh at me coming to such a conclusion.

So, as my mind reluctantly ordered my hands away from my eyes, I looked around and saw a line of eyeballs and mouths. I told you you wouldn't believe me. They were in the right positions, two eyes, a left and a right, over a mouth the right size for the eyes, but nothing surrounding the eyeballs, just . . . eyeballs. More than I could count of these apparitions stretched off into the distance in a long line.

They all appeared to float as if connected to a body, but there were no bodies anywhere. I felt safe, because after all, I was only here as an observer. So long as none of the mouths opened to talk to me, I refused to be alarmed at this weird scene. Me and my big mouth. I knew the silence was too good to be true. Just as the thought that I was safe crossed my mind, one of the "Things" turned to me and began talking. For the time being, I had to call them "Things", because they could hardly be thought of as people, and I didn't know what else to call them.

"Hey lady, are you just going to stand there all night? Don't you have anything to say?" I suddenly realized that if these "Things" had no bodies, then I too must have no body. Now I was really concerned. I looked down, and sure enough, I wasn't there. I mean, I didn't have a body. "Oh, my God," I said out loud. Or at least my disembodied mouth said it. With no ears, I don't know how I was hearing, but I was. "Is that it?" the "Thing" said facetiously. "Another sophisticated conversationalist, wonderful," he sneered. What a jerk. I knew I had to try one more time to see if this was a dream. I was not going to talk to this guy unless I was dead and I had to. Maybe, if I yelled real loud, my husband would hear me and wake me up. So I let out a desperate scream for help. "Steeeeeeeeeeeeeeeeeeeeeeeeeeeeeeeve, HELP!" Silence. "Wake me up! Please help!" When he didn't answer, I remembered that he was given strict orders to not disturb me. Me and my big mouth again. Before my bath, I had told everyone not to disturb me, no matter what I did or said. Isn't it ironic that this was the one time my family chose to listen to me? It seems to work this way for mothers, doesn't it. Once again, my big mouth dug my own grave.

"What are you yelling about, lady? I just asked you a simple question. If you don't want to say anything, you don't have to. Nobody's twisting your arm to be sociable." I thought better of telling him that I didn't have an arm to be twisted. I think the voice was that of either a high-pitched male or a low-pitched female, but it was hard to tell. Then one of the other "Things" looked at me. "C'mon, honey, why don't you join us? We won't hurt you. You don't have to stand there by yourself." "Stand?" I asked myself. This time the voice had sounded as if it was coming from a husky female. It was hard to tell who was what, what was who, and what I was even doing there.

Until I knew whether I was dreaming or dead, I wasn't going to respond to any of these "Things". I have to admit, I was beginning to think I had died, because I don't think I've ever been creative enough to have a dream this complicated or detailed. One good sign, I was up in the clouds, not down wherever. I had always believed that mothers automatically qualified for entrance through the Pearly Gates, as I said before.

I began listening to the other eyes-and-mouths. I wasn't sure, but it sounded like an argument. Each set of eyes-and-mouth was very different, as if they were real people, only without bodies. The more I listened, the more I was able to picture a specific body for each voice. I noticed that our group wasn't alone. I could see many other groups of four sets of eyes-and-mouths forming a line. At the far end of the line stood an old man with a long, white beard. He was writing on a scroll that was so long it unrolled itself from the podium where he stood and curled along the ground (the clouds, I guess I should say). He seemed to be talking to the people at the front of the line, then he would point to something behind him. The "Thing" at the front of the line was crying. Then it moved through a door and just disappeared. The next "Thing" in line started screaming with joy. It then moved through a different door. Nothing was making any sense. The stranger everything got, the more convinced I became that it was all a dream. I knew that before too long I would wake up and everything would be normal again. In the meantime, my group continued to argue among themselves. I noticed the second smallest person in our group, or rather the second smallest eyes-and-mouth, standing directly across from me. I tried to concentrate on what she was saying, but she rambled on and on without saying anything that made much sense. What stood out about her was that she appeared to control two of the "Things" in our group, but not the very smallest "Thing". I am not sure why, but I knew that the controlling "Thing" was a Woman's Woman.

The smallest of the "Things" just stood there with a silly smirk on its mouth. Every once in a while, it would interrupt whoever was speaking. He was truly annoying, a real brat. Again, I knew immediately he was The King, Little Boy Forever. I don't know how I knew this about him or how I suddenly knew about the others in the group, but I knew each of them as well as I knew my own children. The lady with the sultry voice started talking again. "Ten years of marriage made me itchy for what men had and were allowed to do, that women weren't. I decided to go back to school and get an MBA. When I finished school, I started my own business buying gifts for professional people, who were too busy or didn't know enough about the people they were buying gifts for. I became a real Woman's Woman. I didn't need any man in my life. I had them all in the palm of my hand. I found their weaknesses and I'm now raking in a lot of money from them."

Paying no attention to her jabbering, another "Thing" started talking. Nobody cared what any other "Thing" was saying. This particular "Thing" spoke in a deep voice, quarrelsome and arrogant. "You frustrated bitch! If you want my opinion lady, I think all you need is a good lay from a real man like me. If you were my woman, I'd show you your real place in life." I couldn't believe what I was hearing. The Woman's Woman interrupted him. "You men don't understand what advantage women have over men. Women have the best of both worlds, we can be soft like a woman, and hard like a man. All I have to do is dress seductively and your head takes over. And don't think for one second I'm talking about the head on your shoulders. I'm talking about the one between your legs."

"What in the hell are you talking about?" said the Man's Man. "No woman ever controlled me. All I had to do was look at a woman and she was mine. My car, my big house in the hills, my muscular body, these were enough for me to control any chic." This obnoxious, macho, mistake for a real man, was too much for me to listen to anymore. He was really beginning to get under my skin, if I had any skin to get under. This guy had to have come right out of the singles bar scene. I was surprised there weren't any gold chains hanging around his invisible neck. Simultaneously, they all turned and looked at me. There was a long pause. I guess they were all waiting for me to say something.

"Don't look at me like that," I said crossly, uncomfortable under their collective scrutiny. "Don't you have anything to say?" Man's Man asked me, as if he already knew what I should be saying.

That did it. I couldn't hold it in any longer. "I don't want to be put in the position of siding with any of you. As far as I'm concerned, you're all trying to sound like something other than who you really are. As a matter of fact, I don't even know why I'm here, or where here is." They all started laughing at me. Nothing is worse than being in an unfamiliar place and not having any idea why you're there, and then, to top it off, be the butt of some joke you aren't in on. Who knows? Maybe this was a dream, and all dreams were written beforehand by someone, somewhere, just to have fun with us down here on Earth. Think about it. That would be quite a joke, wouldn't it?

"When are any of you going to open your eyes and take a good look at the real world?" asked the Brat, mocking the rest of the group. He took a deep breath. "Take a good look at me, the real me, that is. I am the King, the Little Boy Forever. I wouldn't want any of you to feel stupid, but you're all full of it," He smiled maliciously. "None of you know what you're talking about. My mother was a real woman. She wasn't afraid to admit her limitations as a woman. My father was like all of you. He lived in a fantasy world. He saw women in one way, 'You do for me whatever I ask you to do. You anticipate for me. You are for Me, Me, Me, Me.'"

He paused for a moment, but no one had a comment to make. "I was raised to be just like him. At least with me, you know what you're getting. I am a brat. I'm demanding. I am a little boy, and whether you like it or not, I expect to be mothered by each and every woman in my life. I had the greatest mom in the world. She ran our house as efficiently as a business. She knew how important it was to cater to my every whim."

Another pause. More silence from the other eyes-and-mouths. He went on. "You, the Woman's Woman, you live the biggest lie of all. Either you don't realize it, or you won't admit that the very business you live for is nothing but a woman's typical job in the family. The only difference between you and a real mother is that a real mother is honest with herself. All those feminists always end up taking care of some man in their life, whether they want to admit it or not. It's all a bunch of lies." The Woman's Woman blinked furiously. (The eyeballs had lids, I noticed for the first time.) "Just a minute there, Brat. One very big difference between what I do, and what my mother does, is that I get paid for it. And I don't have to keep on doing it when I get home. Can you comprehend that?"

The Brat just ignored her. Next, he looked over to the Man's Man and started in with him. "Hey, Man's Man, I'll bet you loved being mothered and catered to. A true independent man would not be afraid to be mothered, and could mother someone else right back. You're no better than I am. The only difference between the two of us, is that I'm not afraid to admit I'm a little boy."

The Man's Man ignored him and stared straight ahead. As for me, I was still confused about where I was. But I was sure it was all happening for a reason. Don't things always happen for a reason? I looked up to see what was going on with the rest of the "Things" that were in line. Undoubtedly, sooner or later, I would have a chance to talk to the Old Man and tell him what was bothering me. At least, I assumed that's what everyone was doing up there when they reached the end of the line. The line was getting shorter. How we were moving up, I have no idea, but I was now able to see what was written on the doors behind the old man. Door One read, "Woman's Woman"; Door Two, "Man's Man"; Door Three, "The King, Little Boy Forever" and Door Four, "Eternal Mother Forever." It dawned on me that my group consisted of four people, including me. Three of the four I'd been listening to for the past hour or so. But the Eternal Mother was missing. I looked at the other groups, and for the first time, I noticed that they all had four sets of eyes-and-mouths. That concerned me, because I was obviously the missing piece, the Eternal Mother. It didn't make sense. I was a business woman, a feminist, a Sixties woman, an honorary member of Bra Burners of America. Why me? Without provocation, everyone in my group turned and stared at me again. I hate being stared at, especially when the people staring are silent, and I mean stone dead silent. You know they are all waiting for you to say something, and you don't know what you're supposed to say. "What! What do you want?" I asked crossly, even though I knew very well they weren't going to answer me. Nothing happening made any sense; the weird was becoming the expected.

Imagine for a moment being stared at by a group of eyeballs-and-mouths, knowing they were expecting you to talk to them. Sound normal? Does it make any sense to you?

I didn't think so. Now, here's the real twist. It was becoming logical to me. I was beginning to feel as if I belonged here. I couldn't explain why it was logical, I just felt that it was all right. Obviously, everyone in my group knew who I was, so why was it so hard for me to admit the name given me, Eternal Mother? I had a hard time saying those two words, even in my mind, when I knew they were supposed to be describing me. "What do you want me to say?" I asked again, hoping someone would rescue me from having to talk. I knew that once I started talking, I would be forced to admit, that yes, I was the Eternal Mother and for some reason I was fighting not to give in. Can you tell that I hate confrontation? I'm one of those people who hopes that nasty things will go away eventually, or that someone else will take care of the problem before I have to. Then, as if he could read my mind, the Little Boy Forever began talking to me again.

"Lady, you're so naive. Can't you see what's going on? You are what you are, whether you want to admit it or not. Running away from the truth, won't help you the next time," he smirked. "What do you mean, the next time?" I asked, before I could think about the consequences. I had broken my silence and became a part of this pathetic group. I felt hopelessly lost knowing that whatever direction I turned, no matter what I denied, there would be no escape. There was so much that I wanted to say to the group before I met the old man at the end of the line, and I knew that I didn't have a lot of time to do it. I measured my words carefully before I spoke, and looked at each of the three in turn. I knew exactly what I wanted to say now. "I've spent this entire evening listening to all of you, and all you did was talk about yourselves. Did you actually listen to anyone else? I don't think so. Everything is I, I, I and more I's. Everything is I this and I that. You sound just like my family. Maybe none of you can understand what I'm talking about, but that's okay because I'm going to say what I have to say, no matter what any of you think about me." They all looked at me the way my family does whenever I get angry and am about to explode. "What's she carrying on about?" asked the Man's Man in a bored manner. I could imagine the expression on his face, if he had a face, because he said it just as my husband did when he had no idea what I was talking about, and that seemed to be most of the time. "I don't know," retorted the Little Boy Forever. "She sounds like my mother."

"Maybe you should have listened to your mother," I shot right back at him. "If you had, you would have understood what I said. But no, you're too self-centered, and just said to yourself that she was 'carrying on.' You didn't take any responsibility for anything that happened in your family. You didn't care about why she was frustrated. All of you are so typical, it sickens me." I remember a TV show I used to watch when I was a child called "Queen For A Day". I wish that every male in this world could be turned into a "Mother For A Day". Then maybe they wouldn't take us for granted. Once I got started with this bunch, I became like them. I couldn't stop talking. All these emotions were locked up inside me, and when I started letting them out, there was no stopping me. Suddenly, I realized that everyone was gone, and I was the only one left in the line. Finally, it was my turn to talk to the old man. But where was the justice in leaving my fate to a man? I had catered to men all my life, and here I was again, leaving my destiny to another man. It wasn't fair. Why couldn't he be an old woman? Then I know I would be choosing or being directed to the right door to pass through.

I turned around and saw the old man staring at me, but instead of him looking me straight in the eyes, he looked down at his scroll. Interesting, he was the only one with an entire body up here in the sky. He didn't seem to want to look at me. The mysterious doors were still closed, and I knew I'd have to go through one of them. This time I wanted something different. I wanted a woman to take care of me. This time I wanted to be the Little Boy Forever. In fact, all kinds of women, women like me, could look after me. I would have no cares or woes, because all the mothers in my life would take care of me, the way I do now, for the men in my life. I was beginning to sound as selfish as all the men in my life. It actually was feeling pretty good. At least I thought it did.

I turned to the old man and told him, "This time everything is going to be different. I'm going through that door," and since I couldn't point, I simply looked at it. I told him the reasons for my choice, every great reason I could think of, but he didn't even have the courtesy to look up and acknowledge what I said. He had to be related to my husband, because whenever I make a suggestion to Steve, he never looks at me either. Typical of a man, I guess. Really, I was surprised that he didn't have a TV on his podium with a ball game playing. But eventually, he did look up. He slowly lifted his arm and pointed it at me. I closed my eyes, afraid of which door he was going to order me to go through. I felt I deserved a different life this time. I had paid my dues. I saw no reason to have to go through being a mother to all the little boys again. At last, I forced myself to open my eyes. The old man was pointing to the first door, "Woman's Woman". I looked him in the eye and gave him my famous look, hoping it would work on him too. "I thought I told you I didn't want to be a mother this time."

Fortunately, his arm didn't stop. It slowly moved past each door. I shut my eyes again, and when I finally opened them, he was pointing to door three, "Little Boy Forever". He paused and I felt a sudden rush of excitement. I got my wish.

As I turned to thank him before moving through the door, he started moving his arm again. At first I thought it was a joke, but then I realized he wasn't smiling. On the other hand, I hadn't seen him smile yet. His arm finally stopped on "Eternal Mother Forever". I looked pleadingly at him, hoping he would change his mind. When I realized my inescapable doom, that once you're a mother, you're always a mother. I looked up into the sky and from the bottom most depths of my soul, where joy and pain swelled in quiet hostility, I screamed out "N o o o o o o o o o o o o o o o o o o o! It's not fair! Not again!"

Just like that, I opened my eyes, and woke up. It was only a dream. Only a dream. Thank God. Or maybe I shouldn't be so quick to thank him yet.

MALE FETAL POSITION

CHAPTER 11

It was all just a dream. I knew I should have felt relieved, but I didn't. Instead, I felt confused. I felt my life spinning out of control. I looked slowly around, still half asleep, and began trying to figure out what it all meant. I was in my bed huddled under the covers. I don't think I ever felt more confused about my life, than I did at that moment. That one dream said it all. I moved my pillow against the back of the bed and slowly sat up taking shallow breaths. I closed my eyes again and kicked my feet out from under the covers, still feeling disoriented. I took in a deep breath and held it until I was able to quiet the frustration churning around in my stomach. I couldn't think of any way to make it all go away. I was working too hard. I was trying to be everything to everybody and nothing to myself. Even when I bought a new dress, there was always a reason other than "I want a new dress for me." It was either for my husband or for work, never just for me. Not that I didn't have the desire to buy something just for myself. I just stopped doing it.

Working twenty-four hours a day, at a job I hadn't even been trained for, motherhood, was draining the life force out of me. It was a job I was not unfamiliar with, a job I thought I had wanted, but most of all, a job I was not really prepared for. I never took the time to read the small print in the contract. I am wife to my husband, mother to my children, mother to my husband, a description of me, I was, am, and always will be. To do my job properly, I would have to go on putting my own feelings and needs after those of my family. The problem is, I'm always so busy taking care of my family's needs, I never have time for my own. For years, I have rationalized to myself that it was okay. "Don't worry," I would say to everyone, "They're my pride and joy." I still love my family. I still can call them my pride and joy. But when you don't spend any time taking care of yourself, pretty soon, there'll be no self left to take care of.

Most of my friends chose to get divorced or to have affairs. I chose work and talking to myself. Well, the pressure has been building for a long time now. I've never been one to make waves or bother anyone. When problems arose, I always took the blame. It was just easier that way. It didn't matter to me. I'm always being told by the men in my life what's wrong with me. My mother taught me that any problems in life were always caused by something I had done. All my carefully worked out resolutions to be a good mother—the BEST of mothers—were now making me ill. I was doing everything right, but I was feeling like I was doing everything wrong. It was to the point where I couldn't stand to deal with another one of my husband's problems. I just wanted to go back to when life wasn't so complicated. I wanted to go back to a time when I didn't have to do anything but be a good little girl.

No, wait, that's not exactly correct. That's what got me into that mess in the first place. Now I think I wanted to do something completely uncharacteristic. I also wanted everyone in my home to disappear, even if I felt guilty for feeling that way. Not disappear permanently, of course, just until I wanted to see them again, not when I had to do something for them. When I used to play with my dolls, I could put them away in the closet until I wanted to play with them again, and I knew they were always hidden away and safe. That's how I wished my family could be handled. It wasn't that I didn't love them, I just felt smothered. I'm tired. I looked around the familiar room thinking of my long, complicated dream and still wondered what it really meant. I listened for a moment. I wasn't completely awake yet. Was it the middle of the night? Morning yet? I turned and looked at the clock and I couldn't believe it was only 7:35 PM. The evening was only just beginning. I couldn't even remember getting out of the bathtub and coming to bed. I knew I had to get up. I listened through the walls, as only moms can do. The house was murmuring with the sounds of night. If I listened carefully, I could hear Suzie on her phone, practicing mindless teenage conversation with her friends. I know my daughter. She was having three-way conversation about some boy who would no doubt end up one day being an adult boy. My youngest son Eric, was surely asleep. Steve was the one who usually tucked him in. You could typically find me cleaning up after dinner. That way the dishes didn't sit until the ball game was finished. I was curious about what Steve had done for dinner. I'll bet anything he ordered pizza, then left the mess for me to clean up. It didn't matter whether I had any of the pizza to eat, it still was my responsibility to clean, unless I asked him to do it. This was his version of equality—he ate, I cleaned. It's my fault. I hate a messy sink. He can't understand what's the big deal.

The time had come to go downstairs to see what the boys were up to. I got out of bed, put on my sweats, slowly walked down the stairs, peeked around the corner, and saw Eric sound asleep on the floor. Steve was snoring away on the couch and Bobby was watching some gory movie. Life seemed so simple for them. Bobby looked up, smiled, and whispered, "Hi, Mom," trying not to wake anyone. He looked so sweet. To tell you the truth, they all did. My next step was feeling guilty for carrying on as I had been doing. NO. Nonononnonononononononononononono. NO! I'm not going to let them do it to me again. As I stood watching the boys, I thought about what could be done to be different, but nothing came to mind.

Just as I was about to give in and start the old routine again, the phone rang. It was Michelle, my dearest and oldest friend. I didn't go out with her too much, because Michelle was the friend we all had, who was attracted to trouble, but I think she was just what I needed tonight. She would be a good sounding board for that crazy dream. "Jenny," she said in her usual breathless state of excitement. "I have a great place for us to go tonight. Say you'll come!"

Warily, I asked, "Where? What's doing?" "Oh no, it's a surprise. I don't want to tell you about it now. But I guarantee you'll love it. Come on, be ready in fifteen minutes." I hesitated, then thought, oh what the hell. Let the pizza clean itself up and let them wonder if Mom has really lost her marbles. "Okay," I said cautiously. "What should I wear? How soon will you be here?"

"Anything and fifteen minutes." "See you in fifteen minutes!" I said, and Michelle hung up.

I figured that I was probably in for trouble and that suited me fine. I went back upstairs and dressed in my tightest jeans and a ridiculous glittery Grateful Dead tee shirt. If I was going to play the part of the rogue mother deserting her family without warning, then I might as well dress appropriately for the role. I wasn't worried about the kids, because as long as Steve had his ball game, he wasn't going anywhere. Just as I came back downstairs and went to the den to warn them I'd be going out, the doorbell rang. Steve woke up, Eric continued sleeping, Suzie was still on the phone, and Bobby sat glued to the TV. Nobody moved. Nobody noticed how cool I looked. Nobody wanted to answer the doorbell. Bobby and Steve looked at me with that annoyed look that said "I wasn't answering the door". God forbid they should get up for me. On the other hand, they seemed to have forgotten my storm of a little earlier. It shows just how seriously they take anything I do or say. When I opened the door, I saw Michelle looking stunning, as usual. I think that was one of the reasons I generally felt reluctant to go out with her. No matter how good I thought I looked, she looked better. But tonight I didn't care. I did, but I didn't. You know what I mean? We walked together into the den, and Steve didn't even look up. "Where are you gals going?" he asked, not really listening for an answer. So I didn't give one, and he was satisfied. The game took over his mind. If aliens ever want to take over men on this planet, all they have to do is wait until a sporting event was on TV and no man would ever know the difference, as long as they could continue watching the game. If you wanted to recruit the men of America, just tell them that an enemy force was going to take over all their sporting events and they'd never be able to watch a game again. We'd have the greatest fighting force ever assembled.

"Well, Jen, are you ready?" asked Michelle. "My God, what am I doing? Am I going to regret this?" I asked her, nervously, laughing at the predicament I was getting myself into.

FUTURE WIVES
TRAINING CAMP

CHAPTER 12

As we drove off leaving my life behind, a war between anxiety and exhilaration was banging away inside me. I knew that all I was doing was getting away for a few hours with my bests friend. But I also knew, that without it, I'd go deeper into the doll house world that everyone expected me to live in. How had this happened? Not just overnight, that's for sure. I got all these ideas drilled into my mind starting when I was a little girl. I was expected by everyone to play house. And I loved it. It was fun. It was a dream world and all I had to do was get married and then have it all in the real world. Well, I got it all, and here I am, driving away to get out of my own plastic dreams. It had all made sense when it was a game. Not now though. Not this way. But come to think of it, when I was a child, I could walk away from my doll house world whenever I wanted to. A question occurred to me, do white picket fences exist outside homes to keep people in, or to keep the world out? As we stopped at the end of the street, I looked up and saw that an early moon was rising over the canyon hilltops, telling me that my day had ended. And now, in the moonlight, I had a chance to start again fresh.

I asked Michelle to wait until the moon was fully up over the hills before we continued to wherever we were going. As its cool silver light opened up the heavens and dimmed the evening star, I knew it was now okay.

WOULD YOU MARRY US AND BE OUR SUPERMOM , SO WE CAN GO BACK TO BEING REAL MEN AGAIN?

CHAPTER *13*

"Michelle, now that I left the house without even saying goodbye or cleaning up their dinner mess, where are we going? And it better be as good as you say it is."

"Hold on Jen," Michelle sounded a little annoyed. "Why the hell should you have to do all that? It's a pretty sad day when a woman has to go through that stuff just to go out. I don't know any man that does. When they want to go out with the boys, most of them don't even bother to come home from work. Some of us are lucky even to get a call." She turned and looked at me briefly. "What's the matter, kiddo? Your family can't get along without you for a couple of hours? What an ego you have! Maybe that's why you have so much trouble."

"What do you mean by that?" I asked, "That hurt." I felt I was being betrayed not only by my best friend, who was supposed to be giving me sympathy, but also by another woman, who was supposed to understand the ins and outs of my life from her own experiences. "You sound like either you need them more than they need you, or you bought into their dependence game, and because their lives at home center around you caring for them, you're afraid to hurt the poor babies by letting them fend for themselves for a little while." Michelle paused for moment, shaking her head. "I wish you could hear yourself, Jen. You've convinced yourself that you have to get permission to have any life of your own. Is that why you got married?"

Everything she was saying was making me feel ridiculous and I didn't want to listen to any more criticism. But she was right, I had to admit, but only to myself. "Enough! Let's drop the subject. Now, where are we going? I hope not some singles bar," I demanded.

"No way, Hon. We're going to a lingerie party." She went into a sing-song voice. "We're going to a paaaarty. An all ladies lingerie party." "A what!" I exclaimed, trying not to laugh. I wasn't sure why I wanted to laugh, but here I was, dressed as cool as I've been in a long time, and I was going to a lingerie party for women. It's funny, but I didn't know what to say next. My first night of getting away, in how many years, and I was going to spend it with a bunch of strange women who were going to buy things to satisfy their men. What a joke. An all ladies lingerie party. Oh well, okay, what the hell. I needed a drink. "So, Michelle, how are the kids?" I couldn't believe I just asked that dumb question.

"Jen, one of the rules about going out is that we don't talk too much. Jen, are you asking these questions because you want an answer, or do you just want to talk?" "Come on, Michelle. Do you know them? I mean, have you ever been to one of these parties before? What do we do there?"

"Jen, you're already making this unenjoyable. You sound like my ex-husband. What happened to my best friend from high school? Let go Jen! Just let go!" Before I could think of anything to say to her, Michelle pulled the car up to the curb, turned to me and said, with that same look on her face that always got us into trouble in high school, "We're here."

HURRY HON, THE WATER'S BOILING!

CHAPTER 14

I was surprised. A nice house! A two-story, mission style, painted a dark rose, roofed with deep red tiles. But actually, I don't know what I had expected. I was pretty sure this wasn't going to be some fluffy ladies party. I mean we're looking at sex objects, not plastic containers. I knew what kind of person went to Tupperware parties, but not to . . . whatever this was. Something like this had to be for frustrated or over-sexed and under-satisfied women. There was nothing wrong with my sex life. I mean, Steve and I made love at least once a week. He never complained, at least to me. Halfway up the walk, I stopped to look around and see if there were any other cars, or whether we were the only ones who were going to be at this party. Four cars were parked close together along the curb. "Jen, stop it already! You're ruining my evening before it's even started."

She gave me little push, but I just stood there, rather stupidly I guess. She brushed by me and walked to the unexpected, exquisitely carved door. Now I felt really stupid. I couldn't just stand there by myself.

"Jen," I said to myself, "you make a big deal out of everything. That's why you stopped having fun." I looked up to see where Michelle was. I called to her. "Wait, Michelle. I promise . . . " She turned before she rang the doorbell. "JEN, enough!" She pressed the bell, and the chimes rang faintly inside.

"Okay, I hear you," I sighed. "I promise. I mean . . . " But before I had a chance to finish, the door opened. There stood a woman probably in her mid-to-late forties. She was unexpectedly elegant looking, in a white pants suit. "Michelle, I'm glad you could come," she said pleasantly. Michelle smiled back, stepped forward and said, "I hope you don't mind Marsha, I invited my best friend. Marsha, Jen. Jen, Marsha." "Are you kidding?" Marsha said with a warm smile. "The more the merrier. Don't just stand there, come on in." Marsha led the way. When I saw that the room was filled with other women, I began to relax. They weren't any different from me. They all appeared to be very normal. I don't know why I was so surprised. Come to think of it, I am not sure what I mean by normal, especially the peculiar way my mind has been working lately. However, if they were so normal, what were they doing here? I decided to wander around. I did a quick count, eight women including Michelle, myself and our hostess, Marsha. Some were sitting on the couch, others were standing at a table of beautifully arranged epicurean delicacies. The rest of the ladies were standing near the doorway leading to the living room. I hate situations where I don't know anyone. I had to do something, so I wandered over to the table to try some wine. I picked up a bottle of Chandon Champagne and poured myself a glass. "Hi," a voice said from behind me. I turned around and there was a lady, "Dressed For Success", looking every inch a professional.

"Have you had any experience at this?" she asked, a little nervously, plucking at a button on her navy wool dress. "No, it's all new to me. How about you?"

"The same. By the way, I'm Deborah." She smiled. "Are you a friend of Marsha's?"

"No, I'm friends with the woman over there. She brought me," I replied, pointing to the other side of the room where Michelle was talking to an elderly woman, in her seventies or maybe even older. Next to her was a young girl who didn't look old enough to even be there, except that she was drinking what looked like wine, so she probably was older than she appeared.

"And I'm Jenny. How did you find out about the party,

Deborah?"

"I was coming with a friend too, who'd been here before. She was supposed to meet me here, but at the last minute she canceled and left a message here for me. So I decided, what the hell. I'm already here. Why not? How bad can it be?"

I laughed and told her that I had mixed emotions about it too, and I hadn't even known what would be going on. On the couch, talking and laughing, was a big woman. I don't mean tall big; I mean like BIG, big. She was well dressed in a black and gray striped loose top and billowy black pants, in that chic way that so many big women carry off so well. She had one of those deep, infectious laughs that made everyone laugh just because she was laughing. Even though I didn't know what they were laughing about, I almost joined in and found myself smiling. Then I decided to ignore what people were wearing. This wasn't a fashion show after all. I was beginning to feel under-dressed for the occasion, until I looked back at the youngest woman. She was wearing jeans and a tee shirt too. Why, I don't know, but I was glad she was there. I had the feeling she would make this party fun. She was engrossed in conversation with a woman in her sixties and a very attractive red-head, laughing just as hard.

Suddenly I felt guilty for ignoring Deborah and switched my attention back to her. I noticed that she wasn't wearing a wedding ring. "Excuse me for prying Deborah, but I'm wondering why everyone is here — uh — also I noticed that you're not wearing a wedding ring. I take it you're not married? Are you seeing someone?" "That's funny! I looked at your hand too," she said. "And I was also wondering why you were here?"

Before either one of us got our answer, Marsha walked in. "Let's go, ladies. We're going to get started." Michelle was busy talking on the opposite side of the room so I sat down next to Deborah. She seemed nice enough, and anyway, I didn't want to start all over again introducing and explaining myself. On my left was Deborah, and on my right was the older lady with the great laugh. I felt like I had gone back to the age of six, and it was the first day of school. Michelle was helping Marsha slide a big wooden chest over the floor. God, not a Hope Chest, surely? Obviously, our party was in the chest. Everyone sat waiting quietly, except for the big woman next to me, who was probably very experienced at these things. I don't know why that thought popped into my head. I guess that was one of my biggest problems. I judged people too quickly, sometimes even before being introduced to them. "Well, ladies, it's party time," beamed Marsha.

IT'S A LIST FROM MY MOM. THAT WAY YOU'LL KNOW WHAT TO DO FOR ME WHILE I'M SICK.

CHAPTER 15

Marsha stood by the chest in a way that hinted it held something we all would lust for. She caressed the wood sensually, like I wish Steve would carress me. Her silence aroused even my curiosity. I looked around the room to see if anyone else was as curious as me. Nope. Now I really felt silly. "Ladies," Marsha interrupted my rambling thoughts, "I'm going to bring out feelings in each and every one of you. I'm going to show you toys and clothes that will bring out the child in you, the adult child. You'll create your own fantasies and find ways to arouse your man by your own titillation. You'll bring out emotions and feelings your man never knew he possessed. Arousal and play. He'll be putty in your hands. And you'll bring yourself to a level of sensuality that you didn't know existed. You'll feel a new life in yourself that you may never have known you possessed. If your man won't get up from the TV after he gets home, now he'll start coming home at lunch because he won't be able to put off his passion til dinnertime." I giggled, but thank heaven, so did everyone else. "What if your husband was born without passion?" yelled out the big woman. Everybody cracked up, except Deborah. She was laughing so hard that tears were actually rolling down her cheeks. You could tell that this was a woman who acted like she had never had a sexual problem, but even if she had, she had no trouble joking about it. I was intrigued that Deborah, sitting next to me, not only didn't laugh, she looked annoyed.

"If your lover has no passion, then I have something for the person who is really your best partner anyway, yourself," retorted Marsha, grinning slyly. She'd obviously fielded that question before. Reactions from the group ranged from embarrasment, to outrageous laughter, to denial. Can you guess which one was me? Marsha opened the chest and pulled out an odd-looking object. I knew for sure you could not use this thing in bed, or at least you'd better not try. Then she took out three large rings. "Oh my God, what am I getting myself into?" I thought, still trying to stay inconspicuous.

"What the hell is that?" asked the old lady. "If you think I can use that at my age, you're nuts. If my man sees that thing, he'll have a stroke." She was obviously the type who wasn't going to let a single moment go by as long as she was alive to enjoy whatever her body could still feel. And if it couldn't feel anymore, she'd probably make believe it still could. I was a little jealous. Here was an old lady a lot more than twice my age, who was feistier than I'd ever been, and I still didn't know how to let go and be like her. But I had a feeling I was going to find out.

Marsha went on smoothly. "What I have here is a tension breaker. It's a way of letting go and just having fun."

"Oh really, Marsha?" said Michelle, "If that's what I think it is, it won't just break my tension."

Marsha laughed along with the rest of the group and said, "Don't worry Michelle, it's not what you think it is. It really is going to be fun, trust me. It looks like I don't need much of a tension breaker with this group, but let's do it anyway. Besides, somebody's got to win the prize. This is a ring-toss game. You each get a chance to toss the three rings onto this giant penis."

I have to tell you, I'm really not concerned with playing this silly ring-toss game. My luck, I'll end up winning the prize, and knowing Marsha, it was not going to be a prize I could go home and show my family I won. So what was this prize someone was going to win? I waited for someone to ask, but no one did. They were all too taken up by the oversized thing the rings were to be thrown on. The look on everyone's face, especially Deborah's, were something to behold. She looked really annoyed, and even began getting up to leave.

"Deborah, where are you going?" I asked, knowing very well where she was going. "This is not what I was expecting," she huffed. "I have better things to do with my time than play ring-toss games on a giant penis." "Like what?" I asked. "Like work," she answered quickly, as if she'd rehearsed the answer many times before knowing just how to handle peer pressure. At that moment I realized someone else was truly worse off than me. "C'mon, Deborah, give it a chance." She hesitated, but sat back down—reluctantly of course.

Marsha continued, "As each of you takes your turn, please introduce yourself, then go for it." I learned who the rest of the women were, and to say the least, it was an interesting group. The old lady's name was Dottie, who turned out to have been a professional dancer back in the days of Prohibition. So that's why she was so feisty at eighty-four. Dancers always seem to stay young longer than other people. Her daughter, Bonnie, was sixty-one, and also still very attractive, red-haired and witty. She was the owner of three very successful clothing stores. Dottie's great-grand daughter, Carol, was twenty-one and engaged to be married in three weeks. Carol was dressed in those expensively ragged jeans so much in vogue, the ones with big holes at the knee and elsewhere. Carol was as opposite to her grandmother and great-grandmother as only the young can be.

I've already described Michelle and by this time you should know me. Then there was Madeline. She was great. She really was a walking example of the saying, "Big is beautiful." Madeline was an English teacher in high school and she seemed determined to have fun, even with party poopers like Deborah and me. Finally, Marsha, a very interesting woman. She was an accountant with a husband and three children, like I had. She conducted these parties as a hobby. Apparently, a lot of women out there knew about them, because Deborah told me she did these parties every week. Besides Marsha's drive and energy, she was beautiful. I wondered how she stayed so cool with such an active lifestyle. I mean, here I was in her home, because I was losing it in my home. She had a busier schedule than I had, with just as large a family, so how did she stay so calm?

The rings had now come to Deborah's hands, but she tried to pass them on to me. Perhaps Deborah was just a little too mature for her own good. She'd forgotten how to have fun. To be fair, maybe she never knew how. She gazed at the rings for a moment, and suddenly threw them all together, every one missing the mark. Even though her attitude was beginning to bug me, it was still good to see her do something, because I had the feeling that I was almost as bad, maybe worse in some ways. Marsha picked up the rings and gave them to me. With the first ring, I closed my eyes. Wouldn't you know I made it? The second ring I threw while laughing with everyone. I made that one too. Now I was tied with Dottie. I couldn't believe I was competing with an eighty-four year old, to see who could throw more rings on that giant thing. Either win or lose, I'd be embarrassed. I chose to lose, so I aimed carefully to the side, but like too much in my life, my aim was off, and it plopped right onto the huge, silly penis. I'd won. Everyone started laughing, including Deborah.

They laughed even harder when Marsha pulled the prize out of the chest—a giant vibrator. I flushed with embarrassment, especially when I remembered my small purse. How was I going to hide it going home? I tried to give it away, but nobody wanted it. Dottie said she already had one. And Madeline said she had won one just like it at the last party she'd gone to. The only thing left for me to do was to stuff it under the couch thinking I'd just leave without it.

Well, the party was just starting, and I was embarrassed already. I knew I should have taken my own car. I had no way to leave. I could, of course, go sit in Michelle's car but I wasn't going to do that.

Next, Marsha pulled all kinds of paraphernalia out of the chest. As she began her demonstration of the first object, Deborah interrupted her. "Marsha, this whole thing seems a little ridiculous to me. What we're doing here is trying to spice up our sex lives with our men. Doesn't it seem silly that we're taking the responsibility for exciting them? And all they have to do is just be men."

She stopped and took a breath, looking at the curious things Marsha had just taken from the chest. No one said a word, just waited for her to go on. "I'm not arguing with all these objects. I'm just upset that the load is being put on us for making things better. All he has to do is get hard, and if he doesn't, it's something we're doing and that's wrong. I just got out of a marriage because he expected the perfect wife. We both grew up in good Christian families in the Midwest. The women were taught that the basis of every woman's happiness is to love her husband, and that if she got loved in return, it was because she could arouse it in the man. If the man doesn't love the wife, it's the wife's fault. He must have been aroused before she got married, otherwise why would he had been attracted to her over any other woman? Afterall, we are talking about the male mentality, right?"

Carol, the youngest one there, burst out with, "Oh, I know exactly what you mean! It's all those dumb articles in The Reader's Digest, and all the women's magazines about how the wife can keep her husband happy. I sure as hell have never seen articles in men's magazines telling them how to keep their wives happy!" Everybody laughed at this, coming from a very young woman who seemed to know a lot more at her age than I ever did.

Deborah waited for the laughter to die down, then went on. "Well, so here we are, trying to buy objects and clothes to make our sex lives better. And what are they doing? Probably watching TV or out drinking with the guys, right? Well, not me. I don't ever have to baby a man again. I am NOT going to worry about his ego. I'm not going to put his needs or his pride in front of mine. I don't want family accusing me of being a failure at marriage, because I didn't take care of my husband properly." She gave a rueful little grin. "I seem to be monopolizing things. Sorry!" Marsha grinned back and said, "Welcome to the club, Deborah. That's what you're supposed to do here. Don't worry, we've all done it and we'll get our chance again too. Go on, right ladies?" Dottie nodded sympathetically, remarking, "I whole heartedly agree. Go on, Deborah. Would I be correct in thinking that you've never really got any of this off your chest before?"

That seemed to hit Deborah like a lightning bolt. How could Dottie have known? "Yes. I mean no, I haven't," Deborah continued. "Now it seems like I can't stop!" Since everyone seemed so encouraging, Deborah took a deep breath and plowed on. "Well, when did he worry about my pride? When was the criticism supposed to stop? When would I have to stop excusing his childish outbreaks and criticism of other people? Was I afraid of hurting his feelings or of not being his wonderful, supportive wife?"

I looked over at Michelle and saw her take a nervous breath and began speaking without looking at anyone. "My ex-husband, just like my father was, is, and knowing him, will always be a drinker. We always had to tiptoe around the house out of fear of upsetting my dad. When I was married, the children and I had to hide, to do the same thing with my husband. When has it ever been my turn to be babied, without the condition of letting him inside me as my reward to him for being a good little boy? What I need now is somebody who cares about how I feel. Not just someone who thinks that because he makes a good living and provides for me, that's all it takes to make a great husband. I'm not any man's servant. I refuse to come to him whenever he needs me. Never again."

"That was my point Michelle," Deborah added. "I used to go to him whenever he wanted me. Never again will I do that for any man, no matter how much I want to make him happy. I didn't work this hard to become an attorney to have to cater to some overgrown kid. The problem I have, and I guess the reason I was invited to come here tonight, was that I went the complete opposite route. I started avoiding relationships. Obviously, I make a good living as an attorney. So I got involved with men and thought that money and possessions were fun, but we spent so much time thinking about things and what we were going to do, that I forgot what just simply playing around and having fun was all about. And worst of all, I also forgot the value of just having a man love me for myself. When I was a child, everything was a performance: acting and putting on a good show. This is supposed to be playtime now? My friend pointed out that it's 'things' that get us in trouble in the first place, not love." She stopped and looked with distaste at the assorted toys on the table. "I have to tell you, I'm not finding this a whole lot of fun."

"Deborah, be patient," said Marsha with a look of quiet understanding. "I really do see. I was divorced once and used to feel the same way. These are not just sex things; these are toys that we can use to let go and have fun with. It's not the only way, but it really is fun." Now I understood why Deborah acted the way she did. It was just too bad that she stopped enjoying life in the process. Now that Deborah got all that off her chest, I thought that we could get on with the party. Boy, was I wrong. It was only just getting started.

Madeline jumped right in like it was some woman's grievance committee and it was now her turn. "Deborah, I know just what you mean. I have a lot of fun with my husband. I think it's probably because I do cater to him, and in most ways, he's a good man. But he's still a man. He wanted my whole life to revolve around him. My time, whatever privacy I once had, my own needs, and eventually my soul, became his. I lived my life for him and my children. He wanted to be King. He didn't want to be in the background of my life. Poor baby. Maybe, he didn't want to be looked on as just a paycheck or my future security. If he was supposed to get more from me than I'd bargained for, then I deserved more too—more than being his mother, cook, nurse, or as I used to tell him, his garbage can, so he could dump all his garbage on me and not take it to work the next day. In other words, he'd have to do something in return if he wanted sympathy. How could he expect me to turn off all my own pressures and feelings? And, on top of that, expect me to feel romantic whenever he wanted to have sex with me?"

Wow, that hit close to home. I looked around at the others. It appeared that they were thinking the same thing.

Madeline went on, "One time I even fantasized what it would be like to live as a man. Life would be so simple! All you had to do was leave clothes all over, belch, fart, watch TV, go drinking with your buddies, and in most cases, go to work. That sounded great to me. But I was missing that magical septor between his legs, and I didn't have a catering-wife just for me, so it wasn't the same."

Rather irritated, I asked, "What's so magical about that penis thing, Madeline? I thought all that penis envy stuff went out with Ozzie and Harriet. It isn't the penis itself that's important. It seems to me that it's just something to feel superior about." Marsha spoke up, "Yeah Jen, I agree, the magical septor. But Madeline, what you said about not having a wife just for you, is a lot more to the point." She sighed, "God, just think how terrific it would be to come home after a long, hard day, to one of us rushing around cooking, seeing to the kids, sorting the laundry . . . " She broke off and laughed, "I can see you all know what I mean." Madeline laughed too and said, "Right . . . let me think about this. That didn't come out quite right."

For the first time in awhile Dottie began talking. "As you know, I was a dancer. I must have partied every day until I got married. Then everything changed. Every day started by taking care of the screaming babies, feeding, diapering, cooking, cleaning and everything else a good, obedient wife had to do. Too many days I drooped around the house like a wet rag because I had no time for me. My husband always complained about how I looked, but he didn't realize how much time and effort it took to look pretty for him. And he never paid any attention to the fact that the only time I got help from him was when I asked for it, usually five or six times before he'd move. Why did I have to ask? How hard would it have been for him to offer? In those days, that was almost blasphemy."

"Dottie, that's why I'm here," I interrupted. "You know what I hate? I want to help my husband. I like giving him backrubs, massaging his hair, holding him at night. Don't get me wrong, I really like doing these things. What I hate is, every time I touch him, he thinks it means that I want to have sex. It's like there's some magical agreement between my touch and his erection. What I have to learn to do is when I want affection, I have to talk to the head on his shoulders. When I want to be romantic, you know which head I have to talk to. My problem is, I think my husband has Siamese heads, I can't separate the two." I noticed that every woman was smiling and nodding in agreement.

"I don't want him to think that every time he does chores around the house, he thinks he's doing me a favor by doing my work. He says he'd love to help me, he'd love to massage me, and why don't I just ask? Well, I work all day too. And then I come home to take care of dinner and the house and the kids, and nobody asks me to do all that. Nobody asks me to massage him. Just one time I would love him to just do it without getting an erection."

Bonnie then tackled one of these questions. "Wait, Jenny," she said. "There are two things going on here. First, every physical contact you make, he thinks is an invitation to sex. Right?" I nodded. "Second, you both work outside the home, the same long hours, but everything inside the home is still YOUR work, and so he's helping you with YOUR work, whenever he loads the dishwasher or empties the trash. Right?"

And again I nodded. Bonnie went on, "Jenny, I didn't have an outside job like you when I was married the first time, but I still worked all day. Every day at the end of my husband's working day, he'd come home expecting dinner and waiting for me to cater to all his needs. No matter how many times I tried to explain to my husband how rough my day was, he couldn't comprehend what I was talking about. He insisted that his job was more important than mine. Sometimes he'd play with the kids. He'd toss them around and play games. After all, his day was over, and because he believed my job was not as important as his, there was no reason why my day had to be over too. So, by the time I finished doing everything for everybody else, and needed a little time to just talk to my husband, either he'd be glued to the TV set, or he'd be sound asleep. Do you ladies know what I'm talking about? In fact, he believed if he stayed up a little longer, when I finished doing my stuff around the house, it was time to have sex. When it came to helping me at night, it wasn't his job. Then again, I'm not so sure I even want his help. Did you ever watch a man trying to help?

They work at a completely different rate of speed from ours. Then, when they're finished, they gravitate back to the TV. Even so, I'm always still working while he's resting. It would be okay if his slo-mo pace actually accomplished something, but usually he left more of a mess than there was to begin with."

"Bonnie, I've heard that ridiculous answer too, for why they can't help after work or why he does things in slow motion, as you say," said Michelle. "To them, household duties are unimportant, if they have to do it, but extremely important as long as I have to do it. I think that's what they've learned all their lives. Our work at home is invisible, therefore it doesn't exist or it gets done by elves, not humans, and it doesn't bring home a paycheck to deposit. C'mon, I work at home and at the office. You can't tell me that my office job is less important than any man's job, but I'm a woman, so I'm expected to do both my job and the housework. My husband also had a reason why he was grouchy to us when he got home. He believed that when he came home, he was tired of being on his best behavior for total strangers, and now, thank you very much, he would like to relax and be his true self for his family—the uglier and more torn the tee shirt he put on, the grouchier he was. I often wonder what would happen if I through out all of his torn tee shirts and he was forced to wear nice, clean tee shirts. Would it also force him to be happy? If I went along with his theory, would that mean that all day, because I'm nice to my office co-workers, the supermarket clerks, doctors, teachers, vets, bankers, and everybody else a wife comes in contact with while completing her chores, that I should be grouchy too? I don't think that would ever work for me, because I would never put on one of his tee shirts. No, I'm expected to put on the wifey smile and be happy and sympathetic for him. He might be chronologically older, but I can't see much difference between my responsibilities to him, and to the kids. So finally, I just refused to play his game."

"Why should we have to do it?" Marsha quickly slid into the discussion. "Hey Marsha," interrupted Carol. "I'm not married, but I do live with my fiance. He asked me the same thing you just asked. He wants to know why he should do it. He really doesn't care if it's messy. I thought I'd leave the house messy to see how he'd react. Well, he didn't. He really just doesn't care. He doesn't get on my back if the place is messy or dirty. He thinks, 'so you don't mop the floor, hey, no big deal, don't worry about it, there are more important things to do.' The problem is, I don't really believe him. I think it's just a phase. One clue was that he felt that it was his job to mow the lawn once a week, but he hasn't told me what he thought my job was. I'm waiting for the day he unloads and says, 'Hon, why is the house in such a mess?' I feel like he's setting me up." "Don't worry, Carol. He won't let you down. That day will come, I guarantee you," I told her. "Carol, there's a lot you'll learn about the world that exists on the other side of that white picket fence." "Oh whoopee," Carol smirked. "Jenny, do you know what a perfect woman is?" Dottie asked facetiously. "Way back, long before any of you were born, in the days that you read about in the history books, I was taught to be the perfect woman. Not that I became what I learned, but I was taught by a mother who had lived what she taught. I learned that the perfect wife should hide and forget any of her own emotions, past or present. We learned to expect that our husbands would never understand. We learned to hide our real feelings, even from ourselves, and become picture book females." "It's no wonder most women still can't live without makeup," said Marsha. "At least with makeup we can create any image we need, even the image that helps us feel better for ourselves. I learned to be silent and good in school. I became adored by my teachers, and I guess really more important, boys. We painted a perfect picture of a totally fake world. Don't get me wrong, when I put on makeup it makes me look and feel my best for myself, and yes for him too. I have to admit, I know a lot of women that are lost without their makeup on. Some won't even leave the bedroom without their makeup."

"I became a good girl, a real phony. I learned to play the game. It was so ingrained in my system, that when I got married, I reverted to the image that I'd tried to escape from. My mother had done her work of creation all too well."

"Marsha, what's sad is that nothing's changed over the years," said Madeline, with a flat look obviously meant to disguise her real feelings. "My dad had four girls and one boy, and that one boy was in the middle. Once he had his son, the girls didn't need any more attention or direction. They didn't need anything in Dad's eyes. To him, we just needed to help Mom take care of the house, and get ready to get married and have a family. We didn't need direction in finances; we didn't need direction in any sports. We just didn't need. My youngest sister was affected most of all by my dad's treatment, or rather his lack of treatment. She's now a cop, not a policewoman, a cop. She did it by getting tough and by acting like a boy. As she was growing up, it got worse and worse. Everything she did was for my dad to show him she was the best. It's funny, we had to be the best or we were nothing. My brother, on the other hand, was different. He's a little boy. He lives in his own little fantasy world. So now we have a boy and a girl, both acting like boys are supposed to act, and they've remained like little boys. My brother married the 'perfect little wife', who is happy taking care of her 'perfect little husband'. I worry about my sister. Who will she marry? Where will she find a man to be her perfect wife?"

"But I was different. I always wanted to be a storybook mom—loving, caring and dressed in the most eloquently, beautiful clothes. My friends and I pretended about having babies, changing their diapers, rocking them to sleep, and proudly taking care of our dream husbands. What I didn't realize was that running a household was quite unlike anything we had ever imagined in our doll house world. What I didn't realize was, you couldn't put the babies or the husbands in the closet at the end of the day, and take them out again whenever I felt like seeing them. Being a wife and a mother was a twenty-four hour a day activity, twenty-four hours a day the rest of my young adult life. Something was missing. There had to be something more important and wonderful in all this. After all, women have been doing it since the beginning of time, haven't they?" We all reflected on this question in silence for a moment. I think things were getting a little too deep. Marsha interrupted and said, "Okay, enough for a couple of minutes. Let's take a break. I took out some of my mother's favorite china that she used when she had tea with her friends. I don't know how you ladies feel, but I think we all deserve a little bit of class today." We all got up and stretched. I realized that I was beginning to feel as if I'd known these women for years, not only a couple of hours. I took half of a finger sandwich.

Please don't ask me why only half. I looked over at a platter that had all different kinds of pate on it. I had never eaten pate before and tonight was going to be my first. Since I didn't know the differences between them, I took the first one in front of me, put it on my plate and poured myself a glass of Cabernet.

"I have a question to ask each of you," said Bonnie as we all sat back down in the living room. "Besides Deborah, is there anyone in this room who can honestly say that she doesn't mother the man in her life?" Everyone looked around, but no one spoke. I was surprised. I would have expected one of them to have denied doing it. Bonnie smiled and nodded. "Isn't it interesting that we're all complaining about how our men act like little boys, but we're not doing anything to change it. I wonder why?"

"Maybe you need for them to be that way, more than you need for them to change," said Deborah, sounding annoyed at the conversation. "Deborah, don't act like such a big shot," Dottie retorted, "Are you living with a man now?"

"No, I'm not," she said defensively, "What does that have to do with how I feel about men?" "A lot," Dottie challenged, "It's real easy to say how independent you are and how you will live without a man discounting you. Anybody can run away from a relationship. Let's see if you are still Miss High and Mighty when there's a man permanently in your bed!"

Deborah smiled, not taking offense. "Listen, even though I was married for only a short time, I'm still new at this game. I remember enough about my mother and father's marrige to tell me that I don't want any part of the game-playing, ever again. My mother mothered my father, and my father was the perfect child right back, a man who wanted to be mothered, but he still resented it. She had to take care of all the bills, the houses we bought, fixed our cars and everything else to do with us kids. She ran the house and he was glad she was handling everything. But he would never admit he was glad. Like all men, he loved having a woman take care of him." She paused a moment and looked around the room. We were all listening intently. "My father always felt like he was making the decisions for the whole family. He knew the truth, though. You could see that deep down, he resented my mother for making all the decisions. Yet he never tried to change the situation or himself. He's the same even today. The only difference is, now she's gone, I've taken her place." Deborah nervously laughed. "It's not funny. I became his mother. I took over where my mother left off."

"Deborah, you did what?" shouted Madeline, not believing what she had just heard. "I thought you said you were not living with a man, and that you were never going to take care of another one, ever again." "But he's my father. That's different, and anyway, I can't change him. He's too old and set in his ways."

"Oh, I understand," Madeline said facetiously. "You jump on our backs for having fun and accuse us of whining and complaining, then you have the nerve to say you're different than us. Deborah, there's no difference at all between us, except denial."

"But . . . " Deborah tried to retort. "But nothing," Madeline interrupted. "Why don't you be honest with us; no one's going to hurt you. We're all mothers, some more than others, something we all chose to be. We're not going to change them over night, so let's just have a good time making fun of the poor babies, okay?"

Nobody wanted to speak, Deborah looked at me, smiled, and continued talking as if Madeline had never interrupted her.

"Between the time my parents divorced and today, my father remarried, divorced again, lived with a girlfriend and convinced me to take over my mother's mothering roles. Every time he had a problem he would call me up and I'd always help, even if I was busy doing something else. When I have a problem, I try talking to him, but I get better responses when I stay home and talk to my dog. At least my dog barks when I talk to him. In fact, when I talk to my dog about a serious problem I have, he gets so excited talking back, that he pees on the carpet! Unfortunately, I have to clean it up, so I'm not really sure whether it's better talking to my dad and getting no response or talking to my dog."

"I used to wish I had a dad who thought he was a know-it-all and would give me advice all the time. It would be better than total silence." "No, it wouldn't," Dottie shot back. "Be happy with the blank stares. My father would give me advice even when there was no advice to be given. He would advise so much, that I never had a chance to be heard. My mother would sit there and tell me to 'humor him, he only means well.' Would she humor a friend or a relative who acted that way? No, just the little boy she was married to whose pride she was afraid to hurt."

Deborah heard, but she obviously wasn't interested in what Dottie said to her. Deborah continued talking as if she were the only one there who had something important on her mind. "All he had to do was consider that maybe I had needs too. Any reaction at all would have been great. When he calls me, he expects me to take care of all his problems. Like, 'Oh, I'm so depressed.' He calls me every Saturday morning at nine and tells me 'Are you up'. He doesn't ask me. If he cared what I said, it would be a question, but he doesn't care. He just keeps talking. All he's really concerned about is his problem, so I listen. But when I need him, he's too busy or he gives me his famous blank stare. It's like being the mother of an adolescent. The child never has time for his mother except when he gets in trouble. Then the world has to come to a halt to take care of his problem." Deborah started laughing. "What's so funny?" I asked her. "I don't know. I guess I was picturing my dad. Whenever he was asked to do something around the house, he would make these little boy faces. The pained look would make you think he'd been asked to clean the house from top to bottom like some kind of Victorian slave. Most of the time, he couldn't complete whatever it was he'd been asked to do anyway. My mother would always finish what he started, then he would take credit for doing it. She always let him get away with that. My mom rarely had time for herself. You would think my dad would have shown some appreciation for her. No, instead he had the nerve to say, 'Your mother never wants to do anything fun.' Yeah, of course she didn't. What did he expect? She was always getting the garage door fixed, or a new paint job on a chair that he hadn't finished; or she was busy cooking, cleaning, laundering, listening to all our problems, teaching, bookkeeping, and the list goes on and on. You know what's amazing? After my parents got divorced, my dad accused my mom of treating him like a child. What a joke."

Unfortunately, I knew just what she was talking about. In many ways Deborah was describing my dad. The only difference was that my parents still had a great marriage, or so it seemed to me.

"I grew up very confused," I said, as I was remembering my childhood. "My mother was over-protective. The problem was, I wasn't a little girl. I was a tomboy. I had dolls like other little girls, sure, but they weren't cute, frilly dolls. They were like G.I. Joe type dolls. Any girl dolls I got, I cut their hair off and put them in pants. I did everything the opposite from my girlfriends. I never had the rows of cute little dolls on my shelf. It was probably better that I was like that, because my mother would never have been able to deal with a real girlish daughter."

"When I first got married, I refused to mother my husband, but after the kids were born, he fit right in with them. It was easier to take care of my husband along with the kids. Now he's an eternal child in an adult body. When we got married, my husband said he wanted a wife. But his definition of a wife turned out to be the same as his definition of a mother."

I stopped for a bit, remembering. "One of the things I was most attracted to when we first started dating was his independence. He swore he was different from other men, that he didn't want a mother for a wife. I can't blame him though, because I was looking forward to having a family to take care of. It felt very good taking care of him. Well . . .

he liked it. Why not? I would have loved to have a 'me' taking care of me, wouldn't you? I couldn't think of a better wife for me, than me."

Madeline interrupted: "Isn't that what I was just saying about my sister? Where's she going to find the perfect wife? Where are any of us, for that matter?" Dottie sat up and said, "You're saying that men are going to go on making us pay this price for having a husband, home, and family?" "No Dottie, women are going to do it. Women are going to continue doing it. Once again, the men don't have to do anything, the women will do it all for them."

"I'm not saying anything like that. I'm just saying that maybe every man, woman, and for that matter, child too, shouldn't expect to be waited on by anyone."

"I agree," said Michelle. "When I first met my husband, I set up house for him. It seemed perfectly natural. I became his maid. My work contract was the marriage certificate. What sickens me about myself is that I'm separating from him now and yet I'm still doing his house chores."

I was truly shocked to hear what Michelle had just said. She was my dearest friend, and I thought she was the only woman I knew who would never fit into the traditional wife-mother role. But we were getting used to these bizarre confessions, I guess, because no one jumped on her.

"What gets to me most about my boyfriend is when I get sick," said Carol. "It doesn't matter if it's a headcold or if I'm practically on my death bed. I don't think it's unreasonable to expect a little sympathy, maybe a little comforting and a little caring. Instead, he'll go out with the boys. He'll say, 'I didn't think you wanted me here.' My God, if he's sick and I'm not right there holding his hand, he starts whining. 'You don't love me.' 'Make me some soup.' 'Get me some juice.' 'Fix my pillows.' 'Rub my back.' When he gets a cold, he whines and pouts. He expects me to follow all the rituals his mother followed. He even had his mother send over a list of things for me to do. Naturally, I tore it up. When I tell him how he acts when he's sick, he has no idea what I'm talking about."

"I have to admit that my husband is no different from your boyfriend, Carol," I said, trying to decide which to pick from the hundreds of things I wanted to talk about. "He can be a royal pain whenever he's hurt. It doesn't matter whether he has a headache, back pain, a toothache, or he's just plain sick. He has to make my life miserable, so he knows he's not suffering alone. He's probably a bigger pain to me when he's sick, than the pain he's suffering from. One time he hurt his shoulder. I had to get up at three in the morning to boil what I think is called a hydroculator, or something like that, and then get him ice packs. Then who do you think had to remind him to take his pain pills? And every few hours he wanted me to call the doctor for him. I know it was my fault he acted like that. I didn't have to get up, but his complaining was more aggravating than having to get up. I did it for him the first time, and like a child he expected me to go on doing everything for him from then on. Oh, but when I got sick, he ran to the pharmacy and bought every remedy he could think of. He rushed home and said, 'Take whatever you have to, but please don't be sick.' In the same breath, while I was lying there with a 103 degree fever, he asked me what was for dinner! I pulled the covers over my head, hoping he'd go away, but his hunger drive won out. I think it was more powerful than his sex drive."

I thought for a second and added, "But maybe the television drive was more powerful than either one."

Bonnie looked at me shaking her head in agreement, "I do have the sweetest husband, in many ways," she reflected. "The only difference between my husband and yours Jenny, is that mine gets sick any time he doesn't want to do anything around the house or when I want him to go somewhere with me. First he gets a headache. Then he claims he's getting ulcers when all he has is a stomachache."

Madeline started laughing, "My husband has a weight problem and as a result he has high blood pressure." She said while still laughing, "I'm not laughing about his high blood pressure. I'm laughing at how he acts. He has to take seven pills a day, but because I was worried, I got into the habit of making his doctor's appointments and ordering all his prescriptions. Every morning I have to lay out all his pills. It's become one of my routines. But there are times I've forgotten, and boy does he carry on. 'Where are my pills? You don't care if I die, do you!' Finally, I reached my limit and decided to make him do everything for himself, by himself. The only way I thought I could do it would be to go on strike. I posted a notice on the refrigerator. It said, I'M ON STRIKE, NO MORE COOKING, CLEANING OR LAUNDERING. After a week of eating pizza, KFC and tripping over toys left in the middle of the floor, I ended the strike for my own sake.

They didn't even care about the mess and they loved the food."

"Do you know how frustrating it was to find that out, especially after all the years of slaving over a hot stove to make sure my family had a good home-cooked meal? All the years of picking up, cleaning, vacuuming and mopping to only find out that Ronald McDonald and Chuck E. Cheese were cared about more than me. Afterall, I can't remember the last time one of my kids cheered when they heard they were going home for dinner. One time I thought about wearing a Barney costume while making dinner just to be recognized as somebody special cooking. And I guess they didn't notice the mess and dirt any more than they'd ever noticed a clean house. My family actually thought they'd given me a break; they thought they did me a favor. So I went back to being everyone's mom. I went back to cooking, because they obviously didn't know how to take care of their own health. I was always tired, but especially at night. Now that I look back on that period, I think most of my exhaustion was mental. I didn't want to think. I didn't want to listen. I wanted some guaranteed alone time, but I had to finish taking care of the things around the house. Then, when I went to bed, my husband wanted me to make love to him. Yeah sure, I lost any desire to have sex at all. The thought of being pawed at by my husband, when all day long people were grabbing at me, made me sick. I mean, it literally made me nauseous. I tried to tell him that it was hard for me to get in bed at night, live up to some fantasy of his that he read in one of his men's magazines and also be his wife when I'd been everyone's mother all day long. It was just too hard for me to suddenly switch roles, just because that best friend between his legs was wide awake and ready for action. You know what I mean? It's hard for me to serve up his dinner at seven and then cuddle at eleven. I'm not a programmable machine."

Carol put her hand on her Grandmother's leg and spoke with the typical "it can't happen to me", self confident attitude of a 21 year old. "I don't want to end up like the rest of the women in my family. I mean, at least in the way that they kowtow to their men," said Carol. Madeline asks Carol, "Where did you learn that term?" "I guess my grandmother," she laughed. "I love them dearly, but I don't understand what happened to that free-spirited dancer my great-granny used to be. She did everything for great- grand dad. He'd come home from business and say, 'Dottie, make me a cup of tea.' No 'Hi, how was your day? Good to be home.' Just, 'make me a cup of tea.' She would get up from her chair, after having worked all day cleaning and scrubbing, and then she'd get him his tea. I swore I'd never be like that with any man in my life. I've had enough of women saying, 'don't worry about me, I'm okay,' putting everyone else's needs ahead of their own. Until one day her husband's and family's needs become her needs. My mom, who unfortunately is not here tonight, was in a very serious car accident about five years ago. My dad's love for her really came to the surface while she was in the hospital. He was heart-broken. He promised to do anything under the sun if God would let her recover. He started praying, which was a complete shock to all of us. I'd never seen him pray before. I mean, we all went to church, him too, but he'd either sleep through the service or he'd just sit there with this long-suffering look on his face. My mom and I used to laugh at who looked more in agony, my brother or my dad. Oh, I forgot to mention I have a brother named Phil, a clone of my dad. Their expressions were hysterical. My dad would only go to church because my mother insisted. When she really put her foot down, he did whatever she wanted except, of course, if there was a ball game on TV."

"But when Mom recovered, my dad went right back to his old ways, just like a little kid—out of sight, out of mind. My mom forgave him, though. Even with all his faults, my mom loved him very much. I never understood why, but they had a love for one another that was very special. I only hope my husband and I love each other as much, for as long as my mom and dad have. I just don't want to do it the same way." "Carol," commented Marsha, "maybe they found a formula that most couples are missing nowadays. They sound kind of special. I love my husband, but not like that." "Can you believe how my great grand-daughter talks about me?" Dottie asked, while smiling at Carol's innocence. "I didn't particularly like settling into the life of the typical housewife and mother. But that's how it was in those days. It would have caused more aggravation if I had said, 'No, get it yourself' than if I did it for him. I had no choice, so I became domesticated."

"Things didn't get much better for me as we got older," Dottie continued. "When my husband retired, I had to curtail my social life in order to cater to him. He would say things like, 'Well, it's 12 o'clock, lunchtime. I am retired. I have worked all my life to support you. Now you're supposed to take care of me.' As if I hadn't been taking care of him all those years! And he'd say, 'some days I go out for lunch, but if I'm here at noon, then lunch should be on the table.' The fact that the wife is out shopping, or visiting, or doing housework, or wants to go back to school and take classes, all that is immaterial to his comfort and his routine."

"Why didn't you tell him to leave you alone, or make his own lunch?" asked Deborah. "Because my generation of women just didn't do that. We didn't rock the boat," Dottie responded quickly, as if she had anticipated the question. "Most women of my generation are not afraid of their husbands leaving them, and most of them certainly don't think of doing the leaving themselves and setting up life as a single in their sixties, seventies or eighties. When their husbands retire, those men are generally not very active socially or sexually. They talk incessantly, usually about nothing in particular, but they demand our full attention and they criticize a lot."

"The men usually find that they don't have the friendships that their wives have cultivated. Women are better at friendship; they need it for emotional survival. Men always had their work; women always had their friends. Usually the husband was dependent on his wife for friends. And one of the craziest things about retired men, I should say, one of the things that drove me the craziest, was shopping. Now that my husband was retired and had lots of free time on his hands, he wanted to come shopping with me. Maybe I didn't want him shopping with me. Maybe I didn't want him trying to use his business expertise for shopping that I'd been doing quite satisfactorily for forty years. Maybe I didn't want him telling me how to shop, which was my business. I didn't want him stepping into my territory. It's a very hard time for me and other women. Retirement, that is. I finally reached a point where I'd had enough."

I looked at Dottie feeling a little confused. "Dottie, do you mind if I ask you a personal question?" "No, not at all." She answered. "Are you married? I mean one moment you say, 'my fellow', then you say, 'my husband'. Which is it?" She started to laugh. "Honestly," she answered. "They're one in the same." Carol looked over at her grandmother, clearly surprised at what she was hearing.

"Is there anyone in this room who thinks that things changed for the next generation?" Bonnie asked as she looked at Dottie. "Do you think so, Mom? I've seen enough women afraid to stand up to the men in their lives. I finally had enough. 'Now look here,' I told him. 'We have a problem that we are going to have to resolve. I cannot be your sweetheart, lover and maid. I cannot cater to your every whim. I cannot be your mommy. I cannot do these things for you any more. What about me? When is it my turn? Well, I'll tell you when. Now. Right now, today and tomorrow. Do you hear me?'"

Carol looked at her grandmother, as if to ask, is this true? Bonnie continued, looking for all the world as if the frustration hadn't been overcome yet. "You have to grow up," I told him. "You have to change. You have to learn to help me. I've worked hard all my life too. And now, I'm retired too. Now we're supposed to make a salad together, instead of you waiting for me to do it for you. If I'm going to come home late one day, you could make me a salad. Wouldn't that be great? I'd appreciate it, and it would be good for you and you'd appreciate it too. Doing these things is no big deal, but this is my time as well as yours, so how about making my space as big as yours, okay?"

"What did he have to say to that?" asked Carol. Bonnie smiled at Carol and continued with a tone as if she really didn't mean what she was saying. "Oh, he just mumbled and hemmed and hawed for awhile, but he finally agreed that it did seem fair in the long run." "I'm afraid I haven't seen any changes, Grandma," said Carol. "Well," Bonnie answered, "things have improved somewhat, but he does have relapses, I have to admit. Like when he has nothing to do, he listens in on my phone calls on the extension. He's not sneaky though, he lets us know he's there by butting into the conversation without even knowing what we're talking about."

"That would drive me crazy," I commented, and everyone nodded.

"I lived in a little dream world," Deborah said, breathing out heavily, as if exhaling a bad memory. "It had all been created by my mom, my dad and my husband. It was too easy for me and for everyone else to blame me. I believed that everything was always my fault. I never dreamed of blaming my husband for anything. I took care of him, cooked what he wanted, regardless of what I liked, and of course, I never asked anything of him. I think I was afraid to ask for my needs to be met. I don't mean I was afraid that he would hurt me; I was more afraid of his verbal abuse. He would make me feel small and unimportant. I became very important to him when it was dinner time, but even more so when he wanted sex. He didn't want to make love. I don't think he even knew what the words meant or that he had any idea of how to make love to me. Lovemaking meant he would have to give something and to think about someone else. No, I was just a receptacle for the two minutes of release that he needed to finish his day before he could fall asleep."

"I was the good old middle-class, obedient wife," Deborah continued. "When I left, it wasn't my husband I was sick of. It was me. I divorced my own life because it was lousy. I knew there had to be something better. I just didn't know what. I was surrounded by women clones of me: my mother, aunts, sisters, even my friends. How could I know any better? My husband said he loved me, but that wasn't enough. It was how he loved me that made me feel so hopeless, that made me decide I needed to leave. I ended up not even loving myself."

"Why is it so hard for some men to take care of themselves?" asked Madeline querulously. "It can't be in their genes. What about all those men who live alone—confirmed bachelors and so on, huh?"

Carol laughed in agreement. "Yeah, all the gay guys must have to do all that stuff for themselves." Madeline went on, "My husband, for instance, here's a man who runs a major corporation and I have to make sure he brushes his teeth. I don't mean that he doesn't brush his teeth at all. He's clean and meticulous and a beautiful dresser. It's just that he smokes cigarettes, drinks coffee and his breath stinks. I have to check it every morning before he leaves for work. On the other hand, if he brushes his teeth just before we go to bed, I know he wants sex. When his breath stinks, I know I'm okay for the night."

"Oh yeah," Michelle reflected, "the last three years I was married, my husband wore a clean shirt and tie every day to work. My job was to iron all the shirts on Sunday afternoon. 'You didn't iron the shirts right,' he'd complain. 'I don't like where you put the crease. The collars aren't right. The sleeves aren't right.' Imagine, even if I was sick, he still expected me to do the ironing. One day I got so frustrated with his big mouth and demands, that I flipped out. I ironed decals of really weird stuff on the front and back of all his shirts. I didn't care what he would say. I was sick and tired of him. It wouldn't have been so bad if he had offered to help me while I was doing the laundry. But, because he was a jerk, he got what was coming to him." She looked intoxicatingly happy at the memory.

"Oh God," said Deborah, "I can relate with that. All that ironing of those damned shirts, seven shirts a week. My husband always went to the office for a few hours on Saturday morning too, and then church on Sunday. Once he took off his shirt, he'd never wear it again, even if he'd only worn it for an hour or two. And he wouldn't wear non-iron shirts. He said they were tacky and didn't look right."

Looking puzzled, Carol asked, "What's wrong with sending them out to a laundry? Nobody my age irons anymore and it isn't that expensive to use a laundry."

Carol's grandmother just smiled and said, "You're right, of course, about the ironing. It isn't the particular chore itself, though. It's the idea that anything to do with clothes, or food, or the inside of the house, is woman's work." Carol looked dismayed at this picture and sat quietly digesting the implications. Then the talk shifted gears.

Deborah sighed, smiled nervously and continued as if she

was never interrupted, "I think the fact that I actually walked out on my husband was the hardest thing for him to take," said Deborah, looking a little guilty still for what she had done.

"The night I told him I was leaving him, he looked so helpless. When the divorce was final, and he had to leave the house so that it could be sold, he asked me to come back and pack for him one last time." "And did you?" Carol asked curiously. "I did," said Deborah. "Why?" asked Carol incredulously.

"Because he looked so sad and helpless, I couldn't hurt him anymore than I already had. See, the funny thing is, you can be married to a man of steel and nothing bothers him. But if you ask him to do the hard work around the house, he'll say things like, 'My hip really hurts from the softball game.' He can play softball on Saturdays with a bad hip, but he can't do the yard work. I probably sound like a whiney malcontent, but I did everything from picking up his dirty underwear and socks, to putting his shoes away in the closet. I bitched constantly about it, but I never asked him to pick up his own things. I got tired of doing it all. Finally, I did break down and ask him to pick up his own messes. Would you believe that a few days later, I got a call from his mother asking me why I had decided not to take care of him anymore? I couldn't believe my ears. Actually, I couldn't believe he even told his mother."

"When my husband and I first started dating, he was like this little shadow behind me," said Marsha. "He would come over to my apartment and wait on my doorstep until I arrived home from work. I would tell him, 'I've got to go to the store' or 'I have to run some errands. Give me a little time for myself.' I'd plead with him. He would come in, turn on the TV, and want me to sit next to him and hold his hand. I'd want to relax, go through the mail, check my phone messages. I had things to do. At first I thought I could do both. It even seemed kind of cute to me. I thought if I held his hand for a couple of minutes, he'd let me have some time alone. I couldn't have been more wrong. I had to pull my hand out from his grip with a tug to even go to the bathroom. He'd say, 'Where are you going?' I felt like I was punching a time clock. I felt more crowded with him than I felt with my own children. As the relationship became more serious, he would even follow me into the bathroom. I just wanted a little space, but it was as though he had a hold of my skirt and wouldn't let go. It was hard to tell him to back off; it was like I was rejecting him. I told him, 'You have to learn to do things on your own. You can't be hanging on me all the time.' Now I've set up territorial limits. When we replaced the sofa about three years ago, I intentionally picked out a sectional sofa. When it first came, I said to my husband, 'Great, you can have that end and I can have this end.' Because I set the limits from the start, I was able to claim some space for myself on my end of the couch and I've been able to keep it. When you're in the same room, who's going to run away, right? He can still see me."

Michelle facetiously said, "If I didn't know any better, Marsha, I would have thought you were talking about one of your children." "I am," she said laughing with the rest of us.

O.K. HON THE COMMERCIAL'S ON, TIME TO MAKE LOVE.

YOU'LL HAVE TO WAIT UNTIL THE HOME SHOPPING CLUB IS FINISHED.

CHAPTER 16

"I would love to know who teaches adult men how to cook, can anybody answer that for me? You know they had to take lessons to do what they do, the way they do it. I mean, it's too consistent from man to man. There's no way it could be a coincidence," joked Madeline. "Like, for instance, my husband always burns the bottom of the pan when he cooks and then he just eats the top food. He can't cook anything without burning it. There should be a separate section in the department stores for husband-proof casseroles and pans. I suppose he just tosses whatever he's going to cook in the pot, turns the flame up all the way and the food cooks. But, even when I tell him not to turn the flame up so high, he still does it and leaves it that way. He doesn't seem to be able to grasp the principle of bringing something to the boiling point and then turning it down to simmer. Everything is burned. He just eats the top, and the rest goes in the sink for me to wash."

"At least your husband tries," Carol grumbled. "My fiance can only make things that come in a can, unless I pre-cook for him, put it all in bags, and freeze it for the week or the month. Sounds wonderful, I wish somebody would do that for me. Do you think my fiance appreciates what I have done for him? Yeah right, he complains about having to thaw things out. And what's worse is that when all of that runs out, he goes and buys more canned food."

"If you want a successful comedy on TV, just put the husband in the kitchen cooking dinner, that's all you need. Just let the actor be natural, he'll do the rest. In the real world, a master chef needs good utensils and a good oven. A master husband only needs a telephone and the phone number of some pizza parlor that delivers."

"You're right, Jen!" exclaimed Bonnie. "You just described every man I've ever known. And what about all those bachelors whose fridges just have a couple of six packs of beer and a little something green and moldy, probably not found anywhere else in this solar system? Like the Dirty Harry movies, Clint Eastwood could very easily drop into a store on the way home from work after catching the bad guys and have something good to put into the refrigerator. After all, if Lacey, from Cagney and Lacey, could do all of her policework and then come home and take care of a family, Dirty Harry doesn't have to have a dirty refrigerator."

"Oh yes," said Madeline facetiously, "these are real role models we're seeing on TV and in the movies! How are the guys ever going to get what we're trying to tell them?"

"There's a simple solution," Bonnie said with a touch of sarcasm. "I don't allow my husband in the kitchen. Forget it. He cannot cook. He will not learn to cook and I refuse to have his little green things growing in my refrigerator. I can't fix the car and I sure am not going to learn how. So we have a rule in our house, he doesn't come into the kitchen and I don't go into the garage. I don't need that kind of disaster."

I was fascinated and wanted to continue listening, but I had too many good stories about my Steve. I had to tell them at least one or two. "Okay, ladies. I have one for you. My husband is a gem. Every time I have to do something after work and I can't get home in time to cook the meal, my husband has the cute little habit of taking the kids out for fast food. He just won't cook for them. So I told him, 'Look, don't have that junk tonight. Why don't you try cooking? You're going to end up raiding the refrigerator later anyway, so why don't you cook something?'"

"When I returned later that night, he told me he went into the refrigerator and took out left-over stew, left-over beef and rice dinner, left-over guacamole and mixed it all together. Then he crumbled up a package of Ritz crackers and spread that on the top of his mix and baked the whole thing. When I asked him if the kids would eat it, he said they loved it. You want to know something weird? I tried it and it did taste good. But only a man could concoct such a meal. I could see that Carol was itching to get out her own story, so I said, "Wait, wait, just a little addition to this. The next night, while he was still on the cooking kick, he took five bottles of different salad dressings from the fridge. What a waste of space, he must have decided; let's put them all together, and that's just what he did—Blue cheese, Italian, Thousand Island, Russian, Onion—he sloshed it on a salad and then he had the nerve to give it to the kids. Unbelievable. They loved that too. So I thought, why do I go out of my way to make things that look pleasant? Why not let him cook more often? Probably because there is no way he could continue combining things like that before running out of leftovers or of eventually poisoning us all."

Carol smiled at this tale as if she understood. "One day my fiance was going to make a box of Stove Top Stuffing. He didn't read the instructions. He got out the pot, and he read as far as 'Add 1 cup water and 1 tablespoon butter.' What he didn't realize was that he was supposed to simmer the seasoning with the liquid and then add the stuffing, mix and serve. Instead, he dumped everything into the pot and let it start cooking. Then he read the instructions, but only partly, he strained the bread crumbs, put the water back into the pot and simmered it for six more minutes, then he put the breadcrumbs back in and cooked them some more because he still hadn't finished reading. I got sick to my stomach when I came to the table and saw this inedible goosh and I mean goosh. It looked like some thing they would serve in a 19th century orphanage."

"What did you do?" asked Marsha. "What could I do? I mean, I had to eat it. I didn't want to hurt his feelings."

"Look," said Bonnie with maternal authority in her voice, "I'm sixty-eight years old and I'll tell you that most men can be creative cooks, when they want to be, but they're all slobs in the kitchen. They're very messy. My husband made me a bacon, lettuce and tomato sandwich one night at my mother's house. I thought that poor woman was going to die." Bonnie looked over at Dottie and laughed. "He used what looked like every bowl and pan in the kitchen to make that sandwich. Every time he cooked, it wasn't that it was a problem getting him in the kitchen in the first place, but that he figured since he'd slaved in the kitchen creating this masterpiece, I should be expected to clean up. Believe me, it just wasn't worth it."

"Hmmm," Deborah muttered, "Do you detect some kind of deliberate plot here?"

"I went away for three weeks one time," said Marsha, smiling as she thought about what she was going to say. "My husband hadn't washed a dish in that whole time. There was not one clean pot, cup, glass, whatever, left in the house. I even found toilet paper scrunched in big wads in the sink. Now, can you explain to me what toilet paper was doing in the sink? I was afraid to ask. Half the bathroom towels were there too, scattered all over the place. They weren't even dirty. He loved to cook though. He just refused to clean up anything in the kitchen. He didn't believe in using a measuring cup and then rinsing it out. He'd use it, set it down, and look for another one. If he couldn't find one, he'd get a coffee cup and measure the amount needed for each cup and leave a bunch of those all over the counter after being used just once."

"So what's the ideal solution?" asked Carol. "When men are cooking, should we have edible dishes that can be eaten after being used one time? Knowing my husband though, he'd put the edible dishes in the dishwasher."

"Great idea Carol, but probably a little too expensive," said Michelle. "My husband was a cook in the army. One dish he learned was truly awful. I think he got his orders mixed up. Instead of cooking and serving it to his men, I think he was supposed to cook it and leave it for the enemy. If I had been his commanding officer, I would have had him up on court-martial charges. Well, I was kind of depressed one day and he decided to surprise me by making dinner. The thought was nice, but I had to watch the process so I could be sure I'd survive. I watched him take all these hard-boiled eggs, separate the yolks from the whites, then grate each into white and yellow piles on the counter. Then he dumped about a cup of flour into a frying pan and turned on the heat. No fat of any kind, just flour in a dry pan. Then he started adding water, half a cup, a splash, a cup, then some more splashes, mixing and mixing it up until it was a very lumpy paste and disgustingly thick. He then added the grated egg whites and kept stirring. It just got thicker and thicker. Some more water and lots more stirring. I asked what he was going to do with that dish."

"He stared at it and scratched his curly head. 'I don't understand. That doesn't look quite right,' he admitted. 'No kidding,' I said. So he started thinning it with more water. Well, he had to go from the first frying pan, to a much larger one, because he had to keep adding so much water. 'Honey, what are you going to do with the egg yolks?' I asked. 'I'm going to crumble them all over the top,' he said as if that was the only part of the recipe he was sure of. So he stirred and stirred this horrid mess, as he was sprinkling the yolks on top. They gradually disappeared into the glop.

'You just wait,' he said, hoping this would magically change how it looked. I didn't want to hurt his feelings, even though I knew it might be suicidal. I figured I had to taste it. Maybe if I didn't look, and imagined that I had cooked it, it might taste okay. Girls, was I wrong. It tasted like very old library paste, maybe from a library in a Stephen King novel. You're probably wondering how it tasted. It tasted worse than it even looked. What upset me the most was that he wouldn't even taste it himself. He had the nerve to ask us to eat it, but he wouldn't try it. All he could do was stare at it as if staring would magically transform it into something edible."

"Then my husband said to me, 'Maybe, we should put it in the refrigerator? Maybe, all it needs is to sit overnight.' You should have seen the look on my face. I looked him in the eyes and said, no way will that sit in my refrigerator! That concoction will ooze right out of the container and infect everything in its path. In fact, it almost looks alive now. That won't even go in the garbage disposal. You take that out of my kitchen and put it in the garbage pail, right now! Ladies, I wish you could have seen it for yourself; he walked out the door with his tail between his legs. He was so cute. I didn't know whether to be angry with him or hug him."

We were all laughing, imagining this whole scene. "My ex-husband," said Deborah, "wouldn't eat Oriental food, because he didn't like the names of them. Like Mushroom Chiao—he wouldn't eat it because he thought it sounded funny. You had to call it steak with mushroom gravy for him to eat it. It's the exact same thing, the exact recipe, but he had to call it something different in order to find it palatable."

"Wait, wait. I've got one," Madeline couldn't wait to tell us another culinary tale. "You know I'm married to a junior corporate executive. He's a highly educated and polite man, but a real jokester. He would play tricks on me just to get my attention. Well, one time we'd been fighting for a couple of days, and finally one night we kind of made up. I decided I was going to make him a nice stew. I had the time, because I wasn't working outside the house then. He went into the laundry room to find something. He decided to straighten up the laundry room for me, which was right next to the kitchen. He put some of the laundry products in the kitchen, while he was straightening up. Accidentally, he put a box of bleach away on the staples shelf in the kitchen, instead of where it belonged—on a high shelf in the laundry room—to keep it away from the kids. So here I am making a stew, and you know how you dredge the meat in flour before you brown it? I began cooking the stew by browning the beef, and just then he walked into the kitchen and asked, 'What's that strange smell?' I don't know, I said. I have a cold and I can't smell anything. I'm just cooking the meat. I always do it this way. I dredge it in flour and now I'm browning it. But I had to admit, that even through my cold, it did smell funny."

"I wondered if the meat could have been bad, but it had another odor altogether. I smelled it and he tasted it with one finger. All of a sudden he collapsed on the floor. I started screaming, Jack, Jack, what's the matter? He was just lying there. No response at all. You should know, he has this pivot tooth in the front of his mouth, and if he sucks really hard on it, he can make blood come out of it. He just laid there, and I went into hysterics shaking him, trying to revive him. I still couldn't see any movement. I don't know how he breathed and hid it from me, but I was shaking him thinking he was dead. I started crying, and at that point, would you believe that he squirted blood out of his mouth. Then I really went into hysterics, crying, screaming, Jack! Jack! I tried to pick him up, but of course he was too heavy. I just cried my eyes out. He let me cry for probably, two minutes, before he made any response. I was just getting ready to call 911. Finally, he just sat up and started laughing. He was always doing stuff like that. It was like having another ten year old around the house."

"The only thing my ex ever made came from a can," said Michelle. "When I was around, he'd put the can by the can opener, ask me to open and heat it. I never understood how he got along without me. On weekends I made it very easy for him. I stocked the cupboards with canned meals, I'd prepare extra meals, freeze them in little portions, so I always knew he'd eat right when I couldn't be home for dinner. I don't know if he ever knew how to balance a meal. I don't think he even cared. And I'm sure it's all my fault."

"Our generation was even more extreme than yours ever was," said Dottie. "I have a very dear friend who was a golden boy. He was always babied by every female in his family. He always got everything he wanted. He didn't have a care in the world. All he had to do was sit back and everything got done. When he got married, he had the good sense to marry someone who catered to him in the same way. Any woman who didn't cater to him in his bachelor days, he dumped."
"One Saturday morning I was visiting their house to play

bridge. He got up, walked into the kitchen, took out a jar of instant coffee and shouted to his wife, 'Can you come in here and put the coffee in the cup, so I can add water to it?' My mouth literally dropped open. I couldn't believe what I had just heard. I mean, I catered to my husband, but this went a little too far—no, a lot too far."

"He became quite indignant at my reaction. He couldn't see that he had done anything out of the ordinary. He just couldn't put the teaspoon in the cup, or maybe he just didn't want to. It was a blatant example of a man who wanted his wife to take care of him in all the little, silliest things, so that he could remain a little boy."

Dottie pondered for a moment, and finished by saying, "Do you think that men want women to take care of them, or is it that women want men to stay little boys? Or maybe it's a pattern that gets passed down from generation to generation that we can't seem to change?"

CHAPTER 17

I've always had a hard time with silence. I mention this because there's a depressing lull in the conversation. For some reason, nobody's speaking and it's really bothering me. It's especially annoying now, because my husband is a master with the silent treatment. When he's upset, he can go a whole week without talking to me. My father also tuned me out. He made me feel like it was always my fault, even when I didn't know what I did was wrong. Now everyone's just sitting and waiting for someone else to start talking.

Everyone is sitting in their own world, oblivious to the others, and I'm thinking it's my responsibility to talk. "What in the world are they thinking about?" I thought to myself. I noticed Marsha sitting up as if she had something important to say. She had a look on her face of desperation, as if she was hoping someone would interrupt her feeble attempt of expressing what was on her mind. Deborah was right; the party wasn't much fun yet. But I have to admit, it was interesting. You could feel the strain in the air. Finally, Marsha gathered her courage and broke the quiet. "It scares me that I'm like this," she almost whispered. "I feel out of control, as if I have no choices in life. Even though I'm a successful business woman, I feel like I have no options."

I wanted to ask, "Options for what?" But before I could open my mouth, I realized what a dumb question that would be. I was pretty sure I knew what she meant.

"I think I understand how you feel," said Michelle in a voice void of her usual confidence. "But tell us anyway, Deborah."

"I tried not being a mom to everyone," she continued. "I tried not caring. I tried so hard, but I still felt trapped and bored. It got worse; I found out that my husband had an affair. For a moment, I actually thought there was no purpose in even living. When I was able to bring myself to listen to his reason, I couldn't believe my ears. He had the nerve to tell me that his new woman took better care of him than I had. You can't imagine how that hurt. I tried to make myself numb—mind and heart."

Carol asked in a puzzled voice, "But weren't you furious with him? I'm not hearing anything about anger."

A laugh that was part bitterness and part self-contempt came from Deborah. "Instead of being angry at him, all I could think was, 'What did I do wrong?' Do you hear what I'm saying? I was thinking I had done something wrong. That JERK! Why do so many women immediately blame themselves for every single bad thing that happens in their marriage?"

I had a sudden fleeting memory of an old Mary Tyler Moore episode. Mary had bumped into an empty desk and automatically glanced down at it and said contritely, "Oh, I'm sorry." Why do women have a habit of apologizing for everything, even when it is not their fault?

"I really didn't want to come tonight," said Carol, examining her long, perfectly manicured and painted fingernails. While talking, she looked down at her nails as if she were afraid to join in, or felt that she didn't quite fit in yet. "I didn't believe I belonged here. When my grandmother insisted I come with her, my defenses went up. I didn't believe that we had much in common. Boy, was I wrong."

Bonnie looked up and smiled at Carol with an expression of love rarely shared between the generations. "I think I've just been listening to a frightening story of my future life," Carol continued. "It made me feel helpless, as if I didn't have any choices in life that were acceptable to me. I've read about the great women's libbers of the 60's and 70's, who grew up and seemed to return to the old maternal patterns we're all noted for. Does this mean I should stop trying so hard to live a different life? I mean, if I do change my life, will I eventually fall back into the same old women's ways?"

She stopped a moment, tapped her long pink fingernails on her knees, obviously thinking. "I've tried sometimes to find my way back to my childhood—to a time of sanity, to a time when, even if it didn't make sense, my dreams could make it all better."

"Sometimes, in my late teens," she continued, "I would lie down in my room and remember my doll house. When I was little, it could make everything okay. But I now know, that's the beginning of the denial we all go through. We learn to associate love with taking care of everybody. But where does it start? Why does it start?" She looked around at us, as if we might have answers, and then laughed. "You see, I really wasn't detouring off on some side road. I was thinking about the same thing. Why do we all feel so much responsibility for everyone else and why do we think that's the only reason people—I guess I should say 'men'—will love us?"

"Carol, you're too young to—no, I guess you're not," said Dottie. "Maybe if I'd asked that same question when I was your age, I'd be different today."

"Mother, what the hell are you talking about? In your day they didn't know any better," Bonnie sounded annoyed.

Dottie said primly, "That shows what you know about your own mother." "I was . . . " Dottie started to say.

"You were not Mother, and if I hear that ridiculous story about the roaring '20s again, I'll throw up," Bonnie snapped. "You see? That's what I'm talking about," said Carol. "Even though I haven't had a child yet, I can see how I act with my fiance, I see the way other women in my family act and it scares me. So I'm trying to figure out at what age I became a mother, even without a child. I want to know the exact year. When I was six, twelve, or when? I want to know whose fault it was. Right now, I can tell you I don't want it. What's worse is, I don't even know what the 'it' is."

"No Carol, you're not a real mom yet, but beware of the 'its.' They'll sneak up on you, wrap themselves around you and you'll know just what they are. Then it'll be too late, because they'll already have you in their grip. You finally see them and realize they're all around you. You'll know their roots are so deep, that they can't be cut away. Then, you'll be a full fledged mom."

"Look at me. I'm a good girlfriend and now I'm drowning in my own goodness," said Deborah sounding very cynical. "I can't run, because my shadow is my goodness and my heritage. Have you ever been able to run away from your shadow? Shadows tell stories when you look close enough, even the ones you don't want to be reminded of. I have my own heritage. I don't understand why I keep getting involved with men I always have to rescue. I can't help myself. Unless of course, there aren't any men out there who don't need rescuing. And, if that's true, then I understand why I can't find such a man. Even though my father beat my mother, he needed her desperately . . ."

"To do what?" I interrupted.

"Oh . . . never mind," Deborah answered.

"No, go ahead," I demanded, knowing that she was hiding something important.

"I've worked very hard to become an attorney," she reluctantly continued. "But when I get away from the office,

I feel out of place. I feel like a phony. I feel like I'm trying to be something I'm not." Deborah looked as if life was draining from her. Her creamy rose skin was slowly turning grayish and the shadow of an unidentified pain darkened her eyes. "I only came tonight because my friends have been bugging me to get out at night. They're saying I've been very sarcastic with any male I come in contact with, so I'm here to get away from who they say I am. But they don't understand that I don't want to let go of my anger. I feel safe with it. So what do I do? I don't want to pretend, but after the doll house years of unconditional trust, I feel like I'm pretending, no matter how I act or what I do. I refuse to become one of those spineless moms, who sit around with a bunch of other women, complaining about their lives and never doing anything about them. They don't seem to have any solutions—only questions and problems. I think, they actually do more harm than good. They have to learn to like themselves first, then they can progress. Does anybody know what I'm talking about?"

"Deborah, do you consider yourself a happy person?" I asked.

"Not necessarily, but at least I'm doing something about it."

"Oh, really?" I retorted, more sarcastically than I'd intended. After all, I did feel under attack by this woman I'd never met before. "Yeah, I grew up thinking I was simply there for others. I had no . . . 'me'."

Then Deborah just stopped talking. She appeared to be struggling—not with the words, but with memories. Her eyes were cast down; she seemed unable to look at the other women, as if visual contact would force her to feel something she wanted no part of. I thought, if she allowed herself to feel, she'd break into a million pieces and blow away on the winds of the maleness she hated so much.

I started to lean over to hold her hand to let her know it was okay, but I stopped. I wasn't sure I had the ability, especially when I couldn't reassure myself of the same security I was trying to give her. Deborah slowly looked up, nervously rubbing her hands and began speaking again. "For years I thought it was okay to have sex with my brother. Can you imagine that? I was only ten when it started. I didn't know how to say 'no', because I believed he loved me, like I loved him. But it didn't feel right—every time I tried to tell him how I felt, he put me down. My family always made me feel there was something wrong with me. Me—not him. Why did he? Why me?"

She started crying, trying desperately to hold back her feelings. "One day something inside me just snapped, and I realized I hated his touching me," she continued through her tears. "I thought something was wrong with me for not wanting my brother to touch me. I actually believed what they were telling me, so I held it in. I couldn't take his touch anymore, but it was even worse when he'd tell me there was something wrong with me. So I let him go on doing it."

She paused, took a long drink of her wine and continued. "Strange as it may sound, the anger didn't set in until the day my father raped me after another drunken night. I couldn't believe that my brother betrayed me, by telling my father what he was doing to me. Then my father took it upon himself to do the same. Can you believe my thinking?

I was more upset with my brother's betrayal, than my father raping me. They stole my innocence from my very being. Why have any hope? Why have any dreams? Why have anything of my own? They'll just take it away, I thought."

Looking around at the others in the room, I noticed that several of the ladies were wiping tears from their eyes. Deborah continued, "I was so angry when my dad started kissing me one night, that I wanted to cut his balls off. I felt like his toy—a non-person. One night, when I was only sixteen years old, I helplessly sat at the top of the stairs watching my mom try to persuade my dad, who was uncontrollably drunk again, to go to bed. The more she tried—the angrier he got—the more he beat her. I always knew he hurt her, but I obviously repressed all the memories, until now. I numbed myself to the daily memories of her beatings. I couldn't stand the sight of her pain anymore. I couldn't handle seeing her give so much love and just get beaten in return, over and over again. So I became numb—no anger—just numbness, because I was afraid any display of emotion might result in physical retaliation by my dad."

I slowly looked around the room. There was a deep silence. I could intellectually understand what Deborah was talking about, but I was petrified to feel what she was going through.

"One night I went to tell my mother what my dad was doing to me, but she didn't want to listen. She denied my pain, the same way I had denied hers. I think I hated her at that moment more than I hated my father. I felt that my father and brother had an excuse because they were men, but my mother had the responsibility to protect me no matter what was going on in her life. One day, I came home and found my mother on the couch. Her face was bruised and bloody. My father came into the room and started screaming at me, 'What are you looking at?' Then he started hitting me too. So I began yelling uncontrollably at him. I don't even know what I said. At that point, I didn't care what he would do to me. I didn't care about him anymore. Maybe I was just hoping I would die. So it didn't matter what he did to me. I do remember screaming, 'Keep your .... hands off me!' That was the first time I'd ever talked back to my father."

"My mother came to and started screaming along with me, but for her, it was the instinctive desperation of a mother whose child was being hurt. For the first time, she put her own life on the line for me. 'Stop it, stop, stop, STOP!' she pleaded with him in her own feeble way. For the first time, she was trying to save me. She shrieked the words, while crying and choking on her own blood mixed in with her own desperation. He let go of me for a moment and turned to hit her again. I had the good sense to run outside; I kept running until I got to the park near my home. I sat by my favorite tree, no more than ten yards from the lake and began vomiting. Later that afternoon I went to a friend's house and begged her to let me stay the night. The next day I found out that my mother had been hospitalized. No one ever pressed charges against my father, but at least he left me alone after that—no more rape and no more beatings."

My parents stayed together for a few more years, then he walked out. Ironic, he did the walking and she, to this day, feels abandoned. Can you believe that? At least she doesn't get hit anymore. I won't forget. I don't want to ever.

Can you ladies understand me? I just don't want to forget."

"Deborah," asked Madeline, "why do you take care of him then?"

I could see the tears welling up in her eyes, unwilling to let them come down her cheeks; trying so hard to stay in control as the color returned slowly to her face. I reached for her hand leaving some space to give her the opportunity to reach out in return, or to keep her distance, whichever she wanted. I knew I could give her compassion, even if I couldn't help myself. As odd as it seemed, her pain was giving me comfort in a perverse way. I knew she was okay, even if only a little. She reached out for my hand and held it tight. I was glad and squeezed back, trying to tell her she was okay.

"Cause I feel sorry for him now that he's old," as she took a deep sigh of relief.

DON'T KID YOURSELF.
I'M THE ONE WHO'S
REALLY IN CHARGE.

CHAPTER 18

Deborah's story was so hard to listen to, that no one dared speak. Everyone quietly stood up, moved around, refilled their wine glasses, went to the restroom if needed and sat back down. Deborah looked drained. Yet, there was a certain peace about her face. I was absolutely hooked on this group of women, all strangers to me—except Michelle of course. Our stories were all so different, yet we shared an understanding of one another's feelings that couldn't be explained. They ranged from the ridiculous inept kitchen habits of men, to the tragic brutality of the kind Deborah had just described.

"Why is it so hard for men to talk honestly about their feelings?" Deborah asked, with a serious concern in her voice.

"Oh, I don't know about that," said Madeline. "My husband has no trouble telling me how he feels when he's angry at me. He's so loud the neighbors even know." "Yes, you're right about that," she retorted. "But I don't mean feelings of anger. I mean feelings of love, hurt and caring."

"I don't agree," laughed Madeline, trying to add a little levity to the conversation. "My husband has no trouble telling me about his basic needs and you can smell the results all night long."

"Madeline," said Bonnie with a silly grin, "I've been married for forty-two years and my husband still doesn't know how to express any emotion other than annoyance. No matter what I do, he criticizes me. I'm never right in his eyes. I don't even bother trying to talk to him anymore, because I know he'll just criticize. He always has to be right. It's like talking to a child who knows he never does anything wrong, until he needs my help with something. Then instead of saying he can't do it, he says it's my responsibility, and that if I don't do it and do it right, once again something's wrong with me. It's always something wrong with everyone else—never him."

I decided it was time to join in. "I don't have that problem. If you walk by my desk at work when I'm talking to my husband on the phone, and I ask him to say 'I love you', he says, 'I can't say that.' 'What do you mean, you can't say that?' I ask him. 'I mean I can't say that right here.' 'Why can't you say that?' I ask laughing at him the entire time. I just love making him squirm in front of his friends. The other day he called me and asked if I was in a good mood. 'Why?' I asked him. 'Just answer the question.' 'Yeah, I'm in a really good mood today', I told him. 'Good, I need money.' 'What do you mean, you need money?' I knew we were in trouble. You see, I organize all our finances and keep the records. And that's the one area that we fight over most of all. For example, he puts the little magic card into the ATM, wherever he conveniently finds one to use, and it says, the balance is such and such. He never can remember the simple fact that checks clear twenty-four hours a day now. He thinks, because it says that much money is in the account, that he can take up to that amount out and he doesn't consider what's been written in the checkbook. In fact, he never looks at the checkbook, except to write a new one."

So, this one day he called me at work and said, 'I want money for this, this and this. Can I have it?' I told him that there was no money and that he'd have to wait till payday. He'd spent all the money. He said, 'Oh, c'mon.' So I said, kind of playing out a game, 'Okay, but first tell me you love me.' He said, 'No way. I can't say that here.' 'Yes, you can. C'mon.' 'No way. You know darn well, if I say that, Jack will give me a hard time all day. He just won't let up on me.' We ended up going through a huge argument."

"Eventually, I let him think he got away without saying, 'I love you,' by letting him change the subject, and then when he's ready to hang up, I say, 'So?' 'So what?' he answers, knowing darn well what I wanted. There was no way I was going to let him off that easy. 'So tell me.' Then I get this tiny little whisper, 'Damn it. Okay, love you. Goodbye!' And he bangs the phone down and I laugh, knowing how cute he had to look all embarrassed in front of his friends at work. So you can imagine that, if I can't get any kind of emotion on the phone, except irritation and embarrassment, guess what kind of conversation we have when we make love."

More nods of agreement all round.

"At least he made love to you," said Michelle quietly, a cold anger in her tone. "My ex didn't know what the word love meant. He knew how to have sex with me, like I was a piece of plumbing. We never had any problems with money. I just had trouble with his real wife."

We all looked at her in surprise not understanding what she was talking about. What 'real wife'? We wondered. "He was married to Mrs. Work-and-Money, a lot more than he was married to me. He was like an eight year old playing with his toys. That was his real wife. If I didn't know any better, I'd say he walked around his office all day with an erection thinking about all the money he was making."

"My husband was a very brilliant man. In fact, I'd say he was a genius. But everything he did had to be functional and logical; everything had to have a reason. He was absolutely incapable of spontaneity. You know the old saying, 'Two heads are better than one?' Not true. My husband rarely used the one between his legs, unless we had an appointment. And when we were in bed, he'd focus on his other head. When he was finished, I didn't exist." She laughed at the memory. "But you know something? I think that man would never have left the bedroom if I could have worn a nightgown made out of dollar bills. My eight year old son has the same kind of 'obsession' with his frog. As long as he has his fun, he's happy."

She looked at us, still laughing a little at herself. "What are you all looking at? I suppose you're wondering why I didn't wear lingerie that at least looked like money, right? Because I wanted to be made love to, that's why. Me, not some disguise I had to wear before he'd make love. Well, I finally left him. I had to speak up in my own voice. Until I learned to love myself, I couldn't ever let a man make love to me. So I had to let go of him, to get hold of myself."

"It's funny," said Michelle. "I think men are taught that their penis is a toy and that women should learn to have fun playing with it as much as they do. I'd even go so far as to say, they believe it's a privilege for us to be able to play with it. I think they also believe that it's a really great privilege to have the toy inside us. I just don't know the rules of their game, I guess." This really hit home. I thought of my husband and the way he was about his 'thing'; how much I ought to be honored when it stood tall and ready for action. Funny, Michelle had never shared any of this with me before. This evening was turning out to be valuable in different ways than I'd imagined possible.

I pulled my thoughts back to the present situation and listened to Michelle some more. "My husband tried to teach me the rules of the game by taking me to x-rated movies. He decided that I was completely uneducated as far as sex was concerned, so he was going to teach me—or at least let the sleazy porno movies teach me. We used to go to this really crumby drive-in and watch that stuff. Like clockwork though, about half-way through the movie, he'd always say it was time to go home because I had learned enough. He wouldn't admit he'd had enough. Or should I say, his friend was standing tall, proud and was insisting on getting together with me. Then I became about as important to him as a commercial during a ball game." I tried to imagine what I'd say if Steve tried to drag me to an x-rated drive-in movie, but the scene was so bizarre to contemplate, that I couldn't.

"Do you know what it's like to be engaged to an octopus?" asked Carol. "I can be cooking dinner and I'd swear that he can suddenly sprout eight arms, his hands down my pants, up my blouse, on my chest, my behind and everywhere. No matter what I'm doing, he wants it right now. But if I stop cooking to give into his playing, he'll bitch afterwards that dinner was late. Typical!"

"No big deal," said Marsha. "Let's say I'm lying in bed upstairs reading a book and I hear my husband brushing his teeth before he goes to bed. I know he'll be coming into the bedroom with this silly smile on his face. He thinks he's going to surprise me with romantic moves, but I just lay there and laugh, because it's the only time he really thinks to brush his teeth before bed."

"It's funny," she went on reflectively, "if he hasn't had sex for a couple of days, he can be a real jerk. He just withdraws from me, from everyone in the house. All we get is silence. He won't talk to me at all. He knows that silence drives me crazy so this is a constant battle. I don't respond to him sexually, because there's so little connection, so little intimacy between us. So he pushes sex on me because I'm not responding to him. I don't talk to him after we've had sex because it's so lousy. I feel so put upon; he won't talk to me at all. The whole situation is a real drag. As long as he is getting sex steadily, he can be so nice, just like a little boy having a temper tantrum after being told he can't have a toy and I give in just to shut him up. The angel then shows its devious face. Once again I'm the one who has to give in and that makes me angry."

"Sex for a man is controlled strictly in his head. You know, the one between his legs," said Deborah. "He doesn't have to have any emotion. We're just another one of his playthings. I mean, really, an actual toy. I remember once when I was eighteen. I was coming home from New York City. The train was very crowded—standing room only. This guy put his hand on my butt and I turned and gave him the dirtiest look I could. What gave him the right? What was I, a toy for him to play with, without any invitation or consideration for how I felt? When I stared at him, he had the nerve to leave his hand there and just smile at me. So I turned my head away for a moment, I let him think it was okay. He actually had the nerve to put his hand up my skirt without my permission."

"So, I said to him very quietly, 'Mister, I'll count to three and if your hand isn't back where it belongs, you are going to regret it.' He just kept on smiling. I slowly counted out loud, loud enough that he could hear, but apparently not loud enough for him to do anything about it. I then grabbed his hand, held it over our heads, and screamed, 'Whose freak'n hand is this that's up my dress? Damn pervert! Help!' I'm sure I gave him a thrill though. I'll bet you he went home and told everybody about this girl who just stood there and let him have sex with her in front of everyone. No truth, but a great story for the boys. Once again, I was reduced first to a toy, and then to a great story."

Murmurs went round the circle. I was willing to bet that

every single one of us had experienced the same sort of thing. I certainly had.

"My husband," said Bonnie, "used to only fool around with me during commercials, and still never miss the program. It didn't matter how long the commercial was, he'd always have an orgasm during the one minute commercial. It was as if he had the commercials memorized, so he'd know how long he had to go. He'd then push me away and finish watching the show. But I got back at him. I put the remote control by the bed. When he wanted to fool around, I'd wait until he got inside me. Then I'd grab the remote and turn on the 'Home Shopping Club.'" Everyone was laughing at the picture this made in their minds.

"It didn't stop him," she continued, "which just shows how important any involvement on my part was to his idea of sex. But when I picked up the phone on the bedside table and ordered something from the 'Home Shopping Club' as he was about to come, he blew up. Whew, was he furious. It didn't bother him if I just lay there like a blow-up mannequin, but if I let it be obvious that my mind was engaged somewhere else, he got angry. So now we make love without any commercials. We are a couple again, at least in bed. He loves it when I bring home toys from these parties. When I get home, his eyes are shining; he's so excited waiting to see what fun things I've brought home for him to play with. We still do it while watching TV, but now he pays attention to me. If he doesn't, I always have the 'Home Shopping Club!'"

"I'm eighty-four years old," said Dottie matter-of-factly.

"Before I started coming to these parties, I hadn't made love in over twenty years. At my first party I went crazy buying everything in sight. I didn't care what it cost. I wasn't going to resort to wrapping myself up in plastic wrap, but I was going to find a toy that would make my man's hormones dance like they did when we first met. He had so much fun, that I'm now his love toy. But I don't mind. I bless the little boy in him. I'm sure he has more fun now than the man he used to be ever did."

"This talk about toys and women is not a joke," Deborah said. "My ex-husband would go away on business trips, have fun and there I'd be, at home taking care of everything. I think in his mind I was simply always there for him like an empty canvas waiting to be painted on. He'd tell me how, who, what and where I should be. To this day, I don't know why I listened, except that I had no self-esteem. When he told me he'd had an affair, like it was no big deal, it felt like he had put a knife through my soul. I hurt all over. All I could think of was to ask myself, what were the things I'd done that drove him to it, and why did I do them? I blamed myself. He was the innocent victim. I couldn't believe I was protecting him in the same way I would have protected my own son. But what hurt the most was, he said it was just sex, that she was just another toy. He said he hadn't planned it and that it didn't mean anything to him. How many times had I heard that from over testosteroned men?"

"If it didn't mean anything to him, and he was doing it with her, then what was I? Was I also just a plaything? Was I his mother? All I know is, I hurt. And he had no idea how I felt. No idea at all. When I tried to tell him, he said I shouldn't feel that way and that I was over-reacting. I thought he was right, that I had no business feeling the way I felt. I couldn't even own my own feelings. How do they do it? Or should I say, why do we do it to ourselves?"

"Deborah," said Marsha, "our problem is partly our own. I mean, I don't want to become like my husband, but maybe women are too caught up in being responsible and doing and doing, that we've forgotten how to have fun." "Did you ever notice that little girl games are really rehearsals for becoming women (mothers)? The games are too adult. They wear pretty little dresses. They're taught it is bad to get dirty, like little boys do. They love to play with dolls and doll houses, which are nothing more than pre-mom games. They follow Mom around and learn from their very early years, how to take care of the men in their lives. They don't know any better. They're taught that women are there to look after them, to do for them, even in the games they play. They're not bad, they're cute when they get dirty and Mom has to clean them up. Boys are cute when they get dirty. Girls are cute when they are neat and pretty. Did you ever notice that the men who are all business when they go to parties, don't know how to let go and have fun, are the ones who were never allowed to be little boys? They played responsible games like most girls."

"Then there are the tomboys, the girls who played boys' games. They tend to have sloppy homes; they don't care. They don't grow up feeling responsible for anyone. I'm not sure that extreme is such a good thing either. So, what's the answer? Do we want men to be more like girls and not learn to play? Do we want girls to be more like boys and be less conscious of being so responsible all the time? Or, do we all stay the way we are?"

"Today, I decided not to care any more. Maybe I'll grow a penis, I thought." Michelle said, matter-of-factly.

"You did what?" asked Marsha incredulously, not sure she had heard correctly.

"Not for real," Michelle laughed, "but I felt like I had one. I don't mean I really felt it, I mean . . . you know what I mean. My behavior was almost uncontrollable. I felt like there was a female somewhere in my life who was going to do everything for me. It was an interesting feeling."

"Michelle, are you suggesting that to have fun you have to have a penis and a woman looking after you?"

"No, of course not, Jenny. That's going too far. But even my girlfriends in college who got drunk with the boys, never acted as stupid as the boys did. I once had a boyfriend, that thought he was supposed to act stupid if he was a 'real man.' I'm single now and you have no idea how wonderful it feels to be able to do what I want, when I want, without catering to a man and putting myself second."

"I never had that problem," said Madeline. "Before my husband and I got married, he used to show off his masculinity by farting and belching. The worst was when he farted under the covers and I couldn't get rid of the smell. He believed it was expected of him to do it. He thought it was funny."

"Just acting silly without worrying whether it's proper or not is real good. It would be nice to get my husband to try to act more adult; but I guess it's easier to act like a kid than to suddenly be expected to act like an adult, when you have someone doing it for you all the time."

WHAT'S THE BIG DEAL? IF THE KIDS CAN DO IT, SO CAN I!

CHAPTER 19

"Michelle, you sound a little like you're jealous of the men in your life—are you?" asked Madeline.

"Sometimes," answered Michelle, looking a little confused. "No, not really. Well, maybe, I guess. If I'm jealous of anything, its not the penis. It's what it stands for— expectation that women are expected to take care of the men in their lives. Why do you ask Madeline, are you?"

"Truth?" said Madeline.

"Yeah. I do feel jealous sometimes, but not really for your reasons. I have a very popular husband. He's the great entertainer. Everyone thinks he's a great guy. Every weekend he has an open house. He invites everyone and anyone and I do all the work. He sits and invites; I run around getting everything ready and everyone thinks he's Mr. Wonderful. No one says, I'm the entertainer. Am I jealous? No, I would just love to know how he does it.

Actually, I'm more interested in knowing why I do it. I do know, I don't want him to be a clone of myself. I guess all I want is consideration. I don't want to be the one who always has to think of everything that needs to be done."

Madeline thought for a minute, then went on. "I don't want to have to ask for help. My husband doesn't mind helping, but he never considers doing things like volunteering to drive the carpool for the kids, or clean the oven, or the refrigerator, or sweep the kitchen, or clean the bathroom. Now that I think of it, the only two things I don't have to ask him to clean are his golf clubs and his car. He cleans both of those even when they don't have to be cleaned. Toilet bowls, ovens, refrigerators—these aren't toys. This is another example of my husband's version of doing things fifty-fifty. My husband made a list of all the chores around the house that were important to do. He put down what I thought was important, and then what he thought was important. Now here's the male logic. He said, 'I promise not to ask you to do the chores I think are important and you don't like to do, if you promise not to ask me to do the chores that you think are important, that I don't like to do.' That's why he cleans the cars and I clean the toilets."

"I love my family," Bonnie said this almost apologetically, as if she were betraying the other women for not having something to contribute that was funny about her husband. "I'm not kidding. I really don't mind doing for them. I have to admit I do like making fun of him and all the other men, just like they probably do with us. And I may complain a lot, but it's nice to have a man to come home to, someone who truly loves me."

"You can always buy a cat that will love you and demand far less from you, than a man," joked Deborah. "Maybe so, but I'm a little old-fashioned and I think, maybe, if I keep him a little boy it will make me feel needed. I know I don't want a husband who thinks the way I do. Besides, I don't think there's any way I can change his way of thinking after all these years. So I ask him to help, and I cook, and clean and do everything around the house, and I work part-time, not just for the money, but for my own peace of mind."

"Don't you ladies understand?" said Bonnie sounding a little annoyed. "They just don't think like we do. They even brag that they don't. I'm not putting them down, but even our words are different. Sometimes, I think we're from two different worlds. He looks at me as if the words I'm using don't compute in his male brain. The question is: do they learn to think that way or is it really in their genes? Maybe way back in prehistoric times there were two invading worlds that landed on earth. The two life forms really were completely different. It's the only way I can explain how my husband and all the other men I know, think the way they do."

"Bonnie, I tend to agree with you," I said. "Maybe it's in their genes. There are things that most men don't even think of doing, like we were saying before about cleaning. But it's not just cleaning. He does things that would simply never occur to me to do. Like when he leaves his dirty socks on the dining room table. Its funny, because I don't think when he was growing up he would ever have done that to his mother. I'm not sure if he doesn't think first or if he thinks just completely differently. I'm always after him to pick things up. Like his shoes—there are times when I can find ten pairs of smelly shoes all over the house."

"Speaking of socks," said Madeline. "Every now and then I have to go around the house picking up dirty socks that he forgets to put in the hamper."

"Maybe they're doing it all deliberately to punish us," I said, only half joking. "Maybe they know their wives can't punish them the way their mothers could." Michelle spoke up dryly, "Maybe they're punishing us because they couldn't get back at their own mothers."

"Now there's a thought" I laughed.

"Huh, you should only know from dirt," said Carol. "Our second bathroom has a shower and you have to climb inside to clean it. You can't just turn on the water and scrub it down. In our building the shower and bath seem to have been designed expressly for the purpose of collecting dirt. Knowing my boyfriend, he had something to do with the designing. To give you a good example, I scrub my bathtub every day before I take a shower. No big deal, right? My boyfriend has always used the other bathroom. Right from the start I told him, 'If you're going to use this bathroom and the shower, you've got to keep it clean. You know, when you get out take the wash cloth or scrub brush and wash it down.' Simple request, right? He said, 'Uh huh,' and I figured that was the end of it. But it turned out that I might as well have been talking to him in Chinese. There's no window in his bathroom and as a result the ventilation isn't that good. I never showered in his bathroom, so I never went in. I guess we'd been living there, maybe, two or three months, when I had to go in for something. I couldn't believe the dirt. It was growing! It was as if he was from another solar system and had brought weird, extraterrestrial plants back to earth with him. There were things growing in that bathroom that can't be found anywhere on this planet. There were organisms looking at me that probably wondered who and what I was. A good article for The Enquirer could have come out of it called 'Extraterrestrials live and thrive in boyfriend's bathroom!' I just couldn't believe what I saw and smelled. To say the least, I was extremely upset. At that point, I thought the living arrangement wasn't going to work. I almost canceled our wedding. I could hear him saying, 'You sound just like my mother.' Maybe he was right, but would you want to live with my husband and his bathroom friends the rest of your life?"

"Hey Carol, maybe those life forms are the planet men come from," joked Madeline. Carol looked around the room and burst out laughing when she realized what she'd said. Almost every one of us already lived with that situation. Maybe not organisms in the bathroom, but something similar.

"Carol, welcome to the real world of relationships with men," said Dottie.

I looked at Carol and smiled at the memory of when I was her age. "Remember we were talking about whose responsibility it was to clean? Well, my husband is pretty helpful around the house," I said. "But usually I have to ask him to help out. I shouldn't have to ask. I mean, nobody asks me. I'll give you an example. I get up early in the morning on Saturdays, and by the time he gets up, I've been cleaning for several hours. He'll either be watching TV, reading or out playing golf. If he's around I'll say to him, 'Can you vacuum the living room?' He'll say, 'Sure.' What's the problem you ask? Well, he'll vacuum, then after he's finished, he goes right back to what he was doing. If I ask him to do something else, he gives me a pained look that says, 'I already did what you asked or can you wait until after the game is over?' He thinks he's done his part and all the rest is my responsibility. Not only that, but he doesn't ever empty the vacuum bag and usually leaves the vacuum still plugged in, sitting in the middle of the living room. When he does the vacuuming it's in a straight line. Anything he can't pick up with the vacuum cleaner, he kicks to the side of the room and keeps vacuuming straight ahead. But, as soon as he's finished, he comes back in and tramps his dirty shoes or socks all over the room. When he's done, I have to come in and finish what he didn't do in the first place. I often ask myself, 'Why do I even bother to ask his help?' Maybe I hope that one day he might shock me and do it correctly."

"I had the same problem with my ex-husband leaving his clothes on the floor," said Michelle. "Before we separated, I did something really different to get him to stop. Shortly after we married, we were given the cutest little cat. My husband was, is, and probably will always be, the ultimate slob. His mother had picked up after him all his life. He'd drop things, she'd pick them up and put them away. Every day he'd come home to our little house, take his clothes off, and drop them on the floor. Of course, his mom used to pick them up, so he expected me to do it too, and I did. But not that night. As I said, we had this little cat. I found out that she was peeing on his dirty clothes. I'd feel really bad and wash them. Well, I decided to teach him a lesson. Ladies, I swear this really happened. I ironed his clothes with the pee on them and then hung them up. He got dressed the next day and looked at me like something was wrong, but he was afraid to say anything. Later that day, he called me at work and asked if I had changed detergents. Give me a break— have you ever smelled cat pee? There's nothing like it. There's no way you could think it was a new detergent. When I told him it was cat pee and not detergent, he didn't believe me. To this day he still thinks I put something in the detergent and made up the story. Whatever—he never left his clothes on the floor, ever again. Try it sometime."

"I don't think its fair to blame the men. Even though I admit it's fun," said Marsha, as if she were trying to defend her own behavior.

"Marsha, I've put up with my husband's belittling everything I ever do for so long now, that I feel entitled to one night of not protecting the poor boy's feelings," said Dottie, playing the part of group matriarch.

"The problem is not men and women as such," continued Marsha. "The problem is expectations on both sides. You should watch me run into the bathroom after my husband has trimmed his beard in the sink. I'll scurry in with a rag and cleanser, wipe it all up because we're expecting company any minute. I have to clean the sink after he's trimmed his beard, because all those little whiskers are behind the faucet and all over the sink. When I'm completely done cleaning, he'll come back in and notice that he's missed a few whiskers. He proceeds to trim them and make another mess. Two seconds later, I'm right behind him cleaning the whiskers out of the sink all over again. He thinks I'm obsessive, but he doesn't realize that if it's not clean when the guests arrive, who does it reflect on? Not my husband. It's always me."

"The world expects the woman to do it. It's not fair. If a man, living alone, has a sloppy home, it's okay. It's practically expected. If a woman has a sloppy home, there's something wrong with her. But if a man and a woman live together and the house is a mess, its always her fault. She gets blamed for some kind of character flaw and he gets pitied."

"It's not just men helping or not helping," Madeline interrupted. "My husband works at a completely different pace than I do. I work as if there's not a moment to spare; he moves as if he's someplace else at the same time. Without fail, I'm still working when he finishes. His body then gravitates to the TV."

Without a pause, Marsha jumped in at the moment Madeline finished. We all seemed to be in sync, unlike my conversations with my husband. "One time I was busy doing the dishes when I happened to overhear a conversation my husband had with my son, while they were playing basketball in the driveway. My husband proceeded to tell my son, if he really wanted to make a woman happy, he should never do the cleaning in the house the right way. He told him, that one time when I was sick, he did a perfect job cleaning the house for me, but instead of being happy, I looked around the house trying to find something wrong. 'So,' he said, 'whatever you do, never, ever, do the chores around the house completely right and the woman in your life will be eternally happy.' First of all, let me make one thing very clear ladies, my husband has never cleaned the house or done anything completely right. I always need to finish whatever he does. I was furious. It's a conspiracy and we all fall for it."

"My husband . . ." I jumped in before I forgot what I wanted to say. "He can't stand that we don't have a separate den. I want a nicely decorated room, completely apart from the living room. I put a blanket on the couch because he puts his feet up on it, whether he's got shoes on or not. The couch stinks all the time from his smelly shoes and socks. I'd like to take the blankets off and reupholster the couch. But I know he'll just put his feet up, stink it up and make it dirty all over again. When I sit there, it stays clean. So we have a blanket over the couch, which I hate, but it always stinks and he always sits there the same way. He has his smelly little nest from which he watches television with his shoes, cigarettes and beer cans all around him. The dog lies there with him—dog, beer, cigarettes, tv—man's best friends. It gets worse ladies. My husband and my son sit there and throw this beat up softball all over the living room. They've already broken several small things and I beg him not to do it. I know the next thing to go is the good crystal lamp. They're playing catch and I'm sitting there thinking, 'This is ridiculous. I don't even have one spot in the house I can go to that's neat and clean.'"

"You should see my husband clean," said Bonnie. "At sixty-eight, he acts a like a twelve year old. It's a game to him. But at least he cleans. Most men of my generation never do anything. He loves to run the vacuum cleaner. Anything and everything on the floor he'll go right over—coins, screws, rubber bands, it doesn't matter. Whatever's there, the vacuum will pick it up. When he's done he says, 'See what I've done?' expecting me to be proud of him."

"My husband was the complete opposite," said Marsha. "He was the kind of person who left a trail of clothes wherever he went. Maybe he thought he'd get lost in the house if he couldn't follow the trail of clothes he left. You could follow him through the house because he dropped each piece of clothing as he walked to the bathroom, and if his shoes were sitting there, he'd vacuum around them. He never moved anything or picked it up. And then he only cleaned around what showed. If there was dirt any place that you couldn't see, forget it. He thought like a child, out of sight, out of mind. He'd say, 'Nobody can see it, it doesn't show.' Therefore, to him it wasn't dirty."

"You haven't heard anything yet," I jumped right in again. "There are three males living in my house, and Stanley the dog. Stanley is always the fall guy. He does everything bad. I'll go around asking who did this or that, and the kids always claim their innocence—that includes my husband. I'll say, 'If dad didn't do it, and I didn't do it, and all of you didn't do it, then who did do it?' They all look at the dog and in unison shout 'Stanley!' That means Stanley eats all the cookies, all the chocolate cake and all the goodies in the refrigerator. He's an amazing dog. He messes rooms up that he never goes into. He turns lights on and never turns them off. He leaves the television on, knocks things over and is as much of a slob as my husband. I'll bet you they even have the same astrological signs. True brothers. That's a joke, ladies. I'm being fecetious. Stanley really is quite a nice dog. He's become one of the boys. When we first got, him we took him to obedience school and he did everything right. He even cleaned up after his mess. Now he eats, drinks, sleeps and watches television just like his dad."

HONEY, DID YOU
SEE MY SUIT?

CHAPTER 20

"Have you ever wondered why laundry is typically a female function?" asked Deborah. "I'm not saying that men don't do laundry, but they do it differently from women. Men typically think only about a colored wash and a white wash. The delicate cycle does not exist in the average man's vocabulary. My husband thought the delicate cycle was put on the washing machine to make it more expensive, not for anyone to really use." "That's funny," I said. "My husband determines whether something is delicate by what color it is. For example, if it's pink, it's delicate; if it's brown or black, it can't possibly be delicate. So, when my husband sorts the colored clothes, he puts all the pink and soft colors in one pile, and all the other colors in another; whether the clothes are delicate or not. He has no clue what delicate really means. Do I have to tell you what my delicate clothes look like after my husband washes them? I bought new clothes as often as I bought pantyhose, till I figured out how my husband was doing the wash." I looked over at Deborah and noticed she was beginning to enjoy herself. She was laughing at all the stories now. She jumped in before any of us could tell our stories and said, "The men I've been involved with are not concerned with colors running. My ex-husband had more pink underwear than I did, and mine came from the store that way. 'That's what you get when you try to save time with your wash and mix whites with colors.' His solution was to mix the underwear with jeans. Since he never threw clothes away, I'll bet you he still has rainbow underwear. The funny thing is he was very proud of his creation. Every wash, he tried to change the color of his underwear. Now you understand why I never let him wash my clothes."

"They just don't care," said Bonnie. "Either that or they're too lazy to read the labels on the clothes. I think my husband is more concerned with getting rid of the smell from his clothes, than the dirt. I often catch him spot-washing his clothes; his shirts get washed under the arms and his pants along the crotch. When the dirt gets unbearable to him, he'll ask me to wash them. Can you imagine how perfectly awful they smell?" "At least your husband tries," I said enviously. "My husband believes in the law of fifty/fifty. He thinks it's his job to wear the clothes and it's my job to clean them. Fifty/fifty. He actually said that once, trying to be funny. How the clothes go from his body back to the drawers and the closet, all clean and fresh, is magical to him. It doesn't dawn on him that I have a life too and it's not supposed to be devoted to taking care of that kind of stuff for him. 'You could go to the laundromat,' I tell him. But he always says, 'I don't know how to operate the machines. You don't want me to ruin your clothes, do you?' I'll bet you he used that line on every female he ever had in his life; and you know something—it probably worked. It does for me."

Debbie had a puzzled look on her face. "What's the matter Deborah," I asked. "Why did you ask him to go to the laundromat if he doesn't know how to do the laundry?"

"Simple Deborah, I'm terrified of what he'd do to the laundry room in our home." Everyone laughed, obviously knowing what I meant. "This doesn't say very much for women, does it?" I said out loud to myself.

"My husband offers sometimes to do the laundry," said Marsha, "and as much as I'd love to let him, I'm afraid to think what the results would look like. I even tried a number of times to teach him, not just laundry, but things like cleaning the sinks and the toilet. He just claims that he's allergic to household cleaning stuff, like laundry detergent, toilet cleanser and so on. Or as he put it, 'your housekeeping things.' I told him, if he was allergic to the house, he could always move into a tent in the back yard. He kind of backed down then. But he says his mother never allowed him to do anything in the house, because nobody could do it as well as she could. But I'll bet if he had a sister, she wouldn't have been allowed to sit around and do nothing, while poor old Mom did all the housework."

I digested this in silence and tuned out for a few minutes. I knew most of the women really loved their men, but I had to admit, making fun of men as a group was very therapeutic. I could have talked and laughed like this all night. I was beginning to realize that we all shared these experiences, and my domestic life was just not that important to be constantly worrying about, like I had been recently. It's been fun to laugh for no reason at all.

I spoke up again, "I took my younger son for hernia surgery recently and to have tubes put in his ears. Well, I went Sunday night and pre-admitted him into the pediatric ward. I spent the night at my mother's house because she lives near the hospital and I had to be there at 5:30 the next morning. My husband stayed home with the two older kids, while I was away. My son got discharged at 1:30 the same afternoon and I took him straight home. My husband had been home from Sunday night until Monday afternoon, all he had managed to accomplish was to run the apothecary jars through the dishwasher and a few loads of laundry. I walked in and he said, 'I only have one more load of laundry to do.' I couldn't believe my eyes. He just went around the house, gathered up all the dirty laundry from everywhere and anywhere, including if you can believe, the oily rags from the garage; and dumped it all in one big heap on the floor. He simply crammed the machine full—one load at a time with whatever was on top of the pile—his blue jeans, my panty hose, bras, my daughter's red hand-washable dress, and so on. He'd already put four loads of laundry through the machine, and if I hadn't shown up when I did, he probably would have thrown the panty hose in the dryer too."

"My husband," said Michelle, "my ex, that is, used to put my pantyhose in with his blue jeans, with the zippers still un-zipped. There'd be shredded panty hose hanging out of the zippers of his pants. Then, there was the time he took a very delicate gray sweater of mine—my pride and joy, and put it wet on an old rusty hanger. He hung it up, tore a hole in the sweater, stretched it out of shape and if all that wasn't bad enough, he got rust stains on the shoulders that would never come out. His excuse was that he didn't want to put it in the dryer because it might shrink. So, he thought he'd let it dry on the hanger. I was pretty close to letting him dry on the hanger! I still miss that gray sweater."

"Oh yeah, I know what you mean," Marsha said. "I came home one day and found my husband had done all the laundry. He asked me, kind of casually, 'Oh, by the way, is your green shirt washable?' 'Why?' I asked. 'Because I washed it.' Well, no, it wasn't machine-washable; but of course, he couldn't have been expected to read the label. That poor shirt had gone through the washer and dryer already. If that shirt had been a human being, my husband would have been arrested for crimes against humanity."
"My boyfriend is neat, but he's also a slob," Carol said with a smile, the first I'd seen all night on her face. Even when she laughed she didn't smile. It was as if she were still wearing braces and was embarrassed to let anyone see them. "He's neat about himself, but someone has picked up after him his whole life."

"Yeah, my husband's the same way," said Madeline. "My husband never, ever washed his own clothes. The first few years we were married, his mother came over, or should I say, sneaked over, picked up his clothes and had the audacity to leave my clothes in the hamper. She brought her own laundry basket, took them home, washed them, ironed them, folded them, brought them right back to my house and put them in the right drawers."

"His mother does that?" asked Deborah incredulously. "How can I get her to adopt me?"

I couldn't believe my ears. Deborah was beginning to let loose, that was a joke she told and she even laughed at it.

"Sorry Deborah, you're not a man, you're out of luck," Madeline replied facetiously. "He then has the gall to tell me that he takes care of his own laundry. When we first met, I loved the fact that he was raising two children from his first marriage by himself. The children always had clean clothes, so you can imagine how impressed I was. I would never have dreamed that his mother was doing it all for him. He always wanted his little girl to wear frilly dresses; but he didn't have to wash them, dry them, iron them and hang them up. Mamma did that for him. Their clothes always looked like they were dry cleaned. After they wore their clothes, they put them in the hamper in an organized way. She taught them to sort their clothes before she picked them up, and the next time they needed them they were in their drawers and closets, ironed and ready to go."

"Don't complain, Madeline. At least you don't have to do their laundry," I said.

"I know," she retorted, "but it would be nice if she did mine one day too."

"Have you ever asked her why she does the laundry?" Carol asked.

"No, I'm not supposed to know she's doing it. My husband still wants me to believe he's doing it."

"Well, then, have you asked him why he won't do yours too?"

"He says I'm too picky about how I want my clothes to look, so he doesn't bother because he knows he could never please me. And he's probably right."

"And how many miles does Mom have to go to do this?" asked Michelle.

"Only a couple, but I think she'd travel across the tundra in a dog sled to do it. And she's not a young woman any more. She's so determined to do the laundry for them, that one day, when her car broke down, she took the bus."

"What does your father-in-law say about all this?" I asked still unable to believe my ears.

"I don't know, because I'm not supposed to be in on the secret. But he's just as spoiled as my husband is, so I don't think he cares."

"My husband was the same about everything his mother did," said Michelle. "He was so used to having it all done for him that it was hard to get unused to it. We used to do the laundry at my mother-in-law's, because it was easier than going to the laundromat or laundry room in our apartment building. If the laundry got to my mother-in-law's before I got there, it was usually done long before I ever arrived. I felt absolutely horrible, but it didn't bother her. That was just the way she was. 'It brings me pleasure,' she'd say. And my husband thought nothing of it. You know, I'd say, 'why couldn't you just do it yourself?' You know what he said? 'It brings her pleasure. I want to make her go on feeling needed.' But the whole scene still really bothers me. So I'll give him what I call the easy stuff, that is, just the towels. After all, what can go wrong with towels? All he has to do is throw them in, put in the soap, set the water temperature and size of load, turn it on and take them out. You know, it's not like he has to do any delicates or anything that needs to be hung up. No, he'd just let her do it and I really do think that made her very happy. He was right. It did give her the feeling of being needed by him, and let's not forget, an opportunity to complain about me being a terrible wife and mother. I think all mothers-in-laws like to think that. So at least I was being a good daughter-in-law and gave her a good reason to complain about me."

"Well, I find this very confusing," said Carol. "Each of you would love to have a mother like yourself, taking care of you; but you complain when someone is doing half your work. You wonder why I don't want to be like you?"

"Carol, you misunderstand. If she did everyone's clothes, including mine, I wouldn't mind. But she leaves my clothes for me to do and my husband doesn't say a word. I feel like a leper or something."

"I went out to the laundromat once a week," said Bonnie, getting in her two cents worth before Michelle seemed to be quite finished. "That's all I did because I didn't have a washing machine of my own. He used to think, that if he ran out of clothes, I'd be there to just take care of it. Well, he had another thing coming. I told him, 'You've got to tell me that you need it cleaned. You know, if you wear double sets of clothes every day and double sets of underwear, I need to know. That means I've got to do the laundry sooner.' He would just assume it was going to be done. You know, it would get to be Thursday and he wouldn't have anymore clothes to wear and he'd yell, 'How come I haven't got any more clothes?' He seemed to think that they could go from being dirty to clean with nothing in between except me waving my magic laundry wand over them."

"You know, there are some women who don't pick up after their husbands," said Marsha. "They don't mind living in Slob City. Then, there are some women who are lucky to have live-in help or someone who comes in a couple of times a week. Most of us don't have that luxury and we can't ever live like men do, expecting to be picked up after and have clean, mended clothes appear magically."

"Not all men are like that," said Bonnie. "Some are so clean, they make most women look like messy slobs. You know the type, like Felix in 'The Odd Couple'. The only problem with that type is that they're so fanatical in every area of their lives, that their perfection drives you crazy. Who can live with that? Even Felix's wife couldn't remember? Everything has to follow the book. It's always their way. I think I'd rather live with a slob than with that. You know what I mean?" We all nodded laughing.

"My boyfriend does his laundry, and I do mine," said Carol. "We have a timer on the washing machine that doesn't work a lot of the time. He'll be sitting and watching sports on TV and just forgets about it. The water will overflow in the basement and I'm stuck cleaning it up. But basically, he looks after himself. I don't have to get on his case. I never say anything to nag him, anymore. After awhile, my nagging was more annoying to me, than putting up with his mess. After awhile you just let it be."

"Yeah right, Carol. But you aren't married yet. And you just might find that things will change with that magic piece of paper and a few words from a minister or whatever," I said to her, as if I was her mother.

No one said anything, so I decided to hold my tongue. Carol didn't seem to be all that enthusiastic about the whole business of marriage anyhow.

"I don't know about you two," said Deborah, "but my ex-husband never was and probably never will be able to do his own laundry. You know how some people can't do math or some people have dyslexia? Well, my husband was born with laundrexia. One time when he did the laundry, he stuffed the machine so full that the machine couldn't work even if it wanted to. He thought you just put the clothes in, turn the machine on and it all gets clean. He thought the clothes didn't have to move around, they just have to get wet, soak in the soap and rinse. He has no conception of what goes on in the washing process. When you stuff it that full, the soap doesn't come out. His jeans had little white patches on them from the soap. He pulled them out of the dryer and asked me, 'What happened to my jeans?' Well, that's soap on them. You put too many clothes in the washer and the soap couldn't dissolve and get soaked up evenly by the clothes. 'Is that going to come out?' he asked. I tried washing it out; but I couldn't fully remove it. He blamed me for ruining his jeans, because I never told him he couldn't stuff the machine so full. One time he put something red in with his white tennis shorts, and of course, the shorts came out pink. That's not that uncommon, but he wanted me to go out and buy him another pair of shorts because it was my fault that I made him do the wash when I knew damn well he didn't know what to do."

"I'm married to an executive who has a responsible corporate job," said Marsha. "Lots of people depend on him, but when it comes to laundry, he's completely helpless. One time he called me from the office to tell me he had to go out of town and asked me if I wash some clothes for him? Besides running around doing everything like I normally did, I picked out his clothes and put them in the wash. When he came home, I was busy with the kids, I asked him to put his clothes in the dryer. I proceeded to finish dinner. I started packing for my husband and I remembered his clothes in the dryer. When I opened the door, there was our cat! He shrunk and was wrinkled." I yelled at my husband, 'You idiot, you dried the cat! Why didn't you check the dryer before putting anything in it? What the hell is wrong with you?' You know what he said? 'That's what you get for asking me to do something you should have done yourself; and anyway, the cat shouldn't have been there in the first place.' Then he started laughing and walked away. I don't know which I was angrier at, what he did or what he said."

GARANIMALS
FOR MEN.

CHAPTER 21

Carol looked troubled. "Why do women put themselves through these problems?" she asked the group. "It seems to me we bring the problems on ourselves, then we complain about the results. I mean, I listen to my grandmother tell us how it took her years before she stopped feeling guilty about not being able to take care of her children after they left home. It doesn't make sense that we would want to put ourselves through such aggravation. And no offense to you Grandma, but I don't want to ever feel guilty like you did.

So I ask you, do the women have the men trained, or do the men have the women trained?"

"No one has anyone trained," Bonnie answered matter-of-factly. "I think we all just do what's expected of us and then we wait for what we've done to come out the way we were taught it would. Later, we find out that it doesn't come out the way we expected. I'm sorry to tell you this, but with all the warnings you'll get tonight, you'll probably do it too."

Carol looked up at her grandmother, and for the first time tonight, she had nothing to say.

Marsha contemplated the confusion in Carol's eyes. "Let me put it this way. My husband thinks he rules the roost and yet he's completely dependent on me in the house. It's as if in certain matters, he lacks confidence, either that or he just doesn't care."

"But Marsha, why do you take over the responsibility for him? You treat him like a child and then complain about it later," asked Deborah cuttingly. "Does it make you feel more important? I grew up with two people who made it a science to be dependent on each other. I've been watching my mother and father for a long time. Let's say they're going some place. He stands around looking helpless; he can't decide what to wear. He asks her for advice. She ignores him and lays the clothes out for him before he asks anymore questions. I believe my dad never has to worry about looking good. What's ironic is that most people think he's a good dresser. And they're right; he knows exactly what to wear because he's memorized the combinations that have been purchased for him by my mom. If it's a new combination he's created, before putting it on, he always checks with one of the females in the house to make sure it matches. Why he bothers I never know because it never does. I think we've been dressing him for so long, he doesn't trust himself anymore. I don't think my parents were the only couple in the world with that routine. There's even a commercial on television where the wife is out of town and leaves the responsibility for her husband's care to her teenage daughter. One morning he's rushing around getting ready to go to work and he puts on a tie that doesn't match. The daughter shouts at him from her room to change his tie as if she already knew he would wear the wrong one, before he even came out of his room. She took over the role of her mother so naturally that it was scary to watch."

"Carol, I think we dress them because we're embarrassed to be seen with them when they dress themselves," said Madeline. "You have no idea how many times I tried to let my husband dress himself. I even tried teaching him about style and he couldn't catch on. Either that or he wouldn't. He just didn't think. He'd put on anything without looking to see if it matched whatever else he already had on. He used to put on socks with holes in them to go to work. He thought as long as nobody saw them, what was the difference?"

"The only God-awful things my husband has in his closet, he bought," said Bonnie. "If he goes shopping, I have to make sure any shoes he tries on don't pinch his feet, or I have to check the length of his pants and make sure they're not too short. I have to ask him to stand up and walk around. He usually goes out and buys things four inches too big in the waist and three inches too short in the length. What I want you to understand is I'm not being a surrogate-mom in this marriage. I'm saving myself a lot of work, because he figures I can always fix any problem with his clothes. That's flattering, but it's also a pain in the neck. When he puts on a suit jacket or sport coat, he immediately tries to hug himself, figuring if he can't hug himself, it doesn't fit right. It could hang all wrong from the shoulders or the sleeves could be two inches too short but, if he can hug himself, he'll buy it without another thought. Then, when he gets home, I get the job of doing the tailoring."

"My husband's mother bought his clothes for him even after we were married." I said without hesitation, as if I was reading the lines to a play and it was my cue to talk. "She'd buy these clothes, put them in a supermarket bag and sneak them into the house. She'd never let anybody know what was in the bag. I'd go into the kitchen and she'd pretend she was going to the bathroom. Instead, she would go into our closet and hang up the clothes she bought for him. Then, she'd put the rest of the clothes in his drawers. I was insulted. When I finally caught on to her game, I really got mad. This went on for years. One day I threatened her and it stopped. The problem is, he had to start buying his own clothes. The man couldn't pick out anything for himself. Now that I think of what I fought for, it sickens me. I fought with another woman to see who had mothering rights over the 'little boy.' And all my husband had to do was be 'King child' while his mom and I fought for control. He had a tough life." "You see, that's what I'm talking about," Carol said attacking the whole group, "Who needs those kinds of battles in life? There are enough real ones about serious things. Why do you do it Jenny?"

I just shrugged. "I'm not sure there is an answer. Maybe habit?" A little voice inside my head whispered, maybe stupidity?

"My husband," said Madeline, "still gets up every morning and asks if his tie matches his shirt. One of these days, I'm going to have to sew matching tags inside his clothes so he won't have to bother me anymore. When he went on a business trip, I'd hang his suits in his garment bag. I'd always make sure he had two shirts for each suit because eventually he was going to spill something on one of them. I'd always put the two shirts and a tie for each shirt around the hanger inside the suit they would go with. That way, he'd never get confused. The first time I packed for him, I didn't put the ties on the hangers; I just packed them and he called me long distance to make sure he was wearing the right tie, with the right shirt, for the right suit. 'Should I wear the brown one?' he asked. 'You've got five brown ties, honey. Which brown one are you talking about?' I asked him. I'm sure I sounded annoyed. 'The one with the dots on it,' he asked, sounding like a little boy. Now, unless you knew my husband, you wouldn't appreciate the humor in that question. Dots to him could be a stained tie. It could be color runs. It could be the one with little flowers on it. It could even be diamond shapes or actual dots. To my husband, anything could be dots— anything, as long as it wasn't a stripe. He knows what stripes are. Anything else could be a dot. If there were ever stains on a striped tie, he'd really be confused; he wouldn't know whether the tie was striped or dotted."

"My husband has to look at all his clothes every Monday so he can decide what he will wear for the whole week, said

Bonnie. "The man will go in the closet and agonize for twenty minutes over what he's going to wear. He goes in and paces back and forth. At the end of the twenty minutes he opens the door and asks me to help him. It's a ritual. If it weren't so funny, I probably would go in the closet to help him, but that look of helplessness is so cute, I just can't resist it. 'Which one of these shirts goes with my tennis suit?' he'll ask. `None of them,' I say, teasing him. 'Oh,' he'll say, looking completely confused. He looks like a lost puppy. Then he walks back in the closet. 'I don't understand,' he'll say while standing there scratching his head, not knowing what to do."

"My husband is a perfectionist," said Marsha, interrupting Madeline's train of thought. "I'll hang up all his shirts and things in the closet, and all the rest of his laundry is ironed and put away. He then goes through the closet and says things like, 'this one doesn't fit'; 'I can't button this one'; 'the sleeves are too short on that one'; 'this one needs a button'; and this one has a stain on it.' The clothes he complains about eventually all go back into the dirty clothes hamper; so I don't know which one needs the button for, and which one needs to be washed again. I work just as hard as he does, yet he expects me to go through his things and guess which ones need cleaning and which ones don't fit and which ones need to be mended. Last week I told him, 'If it doesn't fit, throw it away; if it needs a button, put it on my sewing machine; and if it has a stain that won't come out because it's been washed forty times in the last three weeks, throw it out.' Does he listen? No, of course not. He threw it all back in the dirty clothes hamper again for me to take care of it. Then he can't figure out why there's nothing to wear."

"I never had to worry about my husband asking me what matches what," said Michelle. "I made it too simple for him. I went out and bought all his clothes for him. Sometimes, I made him come with me, hoping that through osmosis he'd learn. I eventually gave up because he walked around the stores pouting like a little boy that I forced him to come and I wouldn't let him stay home and watch the stupid ball game."

"I'm sure you've all noticed there are more women in the men's departments of stores, than there are men," Madeline said. "Probably because it's easier for women to do the buying in the first place, than it is to drag the men with them. After I buy the clothes, I go home and put labels in them, so all my husband has to do is look at the labels and match them. On Sundays, while he watches sports, he's allowed to mix and match on his own. He's just not allowed to be seen in public. It's interesting how he always knows what doesn't match. Wouldn't it make sense, that if he knows what doesn't match, he logically should be able to figure out what does match? I tell him that all he has to do is pick out the opposite of what he thinks matches, and it probably will. He doesn't believe he looks like a slob. It doesn't matter anymore; as long as he looks at the labels and stays in the right section of the closet, he'll always look good."

"You know all of this sounds really pitiful," said Deborah, shaking her head in disbelief "Is this what women's liberation has been all about? I doubt it."

Before she could go on, Madeline jumped in again. "Hold on one second lady. I don't appreciate what you just said. I really like having everyone in my family needing me. I wouldn't ever want to be a man; although, it would certainly be nice to have a wife around the house like me. Sure, I think a lot of the things I do are a little absurd, but I'm proud of the kind of mother I am. And I like taking care of my husband and children. So, I spoil him. So what? He really loves me. And that's nice. He's a cuddly little boy. Actually, at 6' 4", I wouldn't consider him little, but to watch him act like a little boy is cute. When I come to these parties, sure I make fun of him. But I buy this stuff because, well that's obvious, isn't it? I'm not putting my husband down. I'm just laughing at him, but I wouldn't trade him for any man in the world. He's loving and tender and I love it when he plays with my hair and sneaks up and massages my back, while I do the dishes. I love it that he needs me, because I really do need him, too."

"Now Deborah," she continued. "I've wasted enough time with that nice stuff. It's a lot more enjoyable poking fun at him than arguing with you about why I mother my man. I'll take being married to my cute, dependent husband, compared to being a hard ass like you and not having any man. At least I have a man that loves me. Sorry, that's how I feel. So, if you don't want to join in, why don't you leave?" Madeline took a deep breath, then smiled at Deborah.

We all looked at Deborah wondering if she might leave, but the look of slight anger had passed over her face while Madeline was talking. "Oh, what the hell," said Deborah, not caring anymore. "You're right about your situation, but I don't agree that a lot of this applies to me. My ex was the most eloquent dresser. In fact, I don't date anyone that isn't beautifully dressed all the time. If anything, they help me pick out my clothes. I refuse to be with anyone that reminds me of my father. So I guess you might say, everyone's entitled to her own right or wrong," she grinned cheerfully at Madeline, who grinned back. Now the evening was starting to get fun.

CHAPTER 22

Madeline took over again. "Enough with the clothes. My feeling is that men should be born with the instinct to clean bathrooms. We pass the genes on to girls, why not the boys? My husband says, 'Because God's a man, and men don't betray other men; so he gives the gene to women. God obviously, doesn't have the gene. Could you imagine God cleaning a bathroom?'"

"Why don't men know that bathrooms are to be cleaned before and after they use them? Afterall, they usually make more of a mess in the sink than women do. Of course, my husband doesn't agree. There's definitely no argument when it comes to the toilet. No woman can ever make as much of a mess in the toilet as a man. My husband's excuse is that he's half asleep when he goes to the bathroom. He says, 'How do you expect me to know whether I'm missing or hitting?'"

"I know just what you mean," said Carol. "Why do they always leave the toilet seat up? In the middle of the night when I'm half asleep, I'll slowly lower my bottom not thinking the obvious would happen. It's funny, my bottom seems to know the seat's not there, because it sends a rush of adrenaline to my brain to warn me as I lower myself that extra one inch to the cold, and probably, wet porcelain bowl. Unfortunately, I'm usually seated by the time I realize what I've done. You know what's amazing? I've never fallen in. I think if that ever happens, I'll sue for abuse of some kind."

"Carol, at least you don't sit on a toilet seat that he's peed on because he forgot to pick the seat up and didn't even know it was down," said Madeline.

"I don't know how my husband manages to do it, but it doesn't matter whether he's hit the toilet or missed, it still smells," I said. "I think they should clean the toilet. Why should I clean his mess? I never miss. I sit down every time and have no problem. I can't even aim the way he can, as he always takes such pleasure in telling me. So why should he ever miss, let alone miss half the time? He wears contacts so, when he wakes up in the middle of the night, he can't see very well. He tells me, 'Be sure you leave the seat up when you get done because I don't know if the seat is up or down.' I guess the lack of contacts makes his hands go numb too and it would be impossible for him to feel whether the seats up or down," I said sarcastically. "I'll hear him get up to go to the bathroom, but I'm not hearing that tinkle, tinkle, tinkle, and I'm thinking, 'What's going on?' Sure enough, he didn't raise the seat; there's no sound and he's thinking 'something's not right here'. He lifts his head and yells, 'AYIEEE!' That's right, he got the whole toilet seat cover sopping wet. That cover has been washed more than my youngest child's underwear."

"Talking about toilet seats, that reminds me," said Marsha. "I have this Great Dane—a very large one. He has the habit, like a lot of dogs, of drinking out of the toilet. It's the perfect height for him. In fact, he believes it was made for him, so I really have two children in the house. When I get up in the morning, I'll go into the bathroom and I'll see my dog drinking out of the toilet. Now, I know that my husband never flushes the toilet in the middle of the night. He also has the nasty habit of flicking cigarettes into the toilet bowl too. So there the crazy dog is, drinking out of the toilet with pee in it, sodden cigarettes floating around, and I have to go to the bathroom. What a scene. No matter how many times I tell my husband to flush it, he always forgets. Poor dog, poor me."

"I think my husband's improving now, but he's not there quite yet. I'll be sitting in the living room and he'll be in the bathroom peeing. The next thing I know, he's flushed the toilet, but he hasn't finished peeing yet. He's still doing it after he's flushed. Then it sits there until I flush it. Once again, the responsibility was left up to me. Where is it written that it's my responsibility even to flush the toilet for other people, once they're over four or five years old?"

WHEN I SAY 'I DO' I HOPE HE DOESN'T EXPECT ME TO DO EVERYTHING FOR HIM.

WHEN I SAY 'I DO' I WONDER WHAT SHE EXPECTS ME TO DO?

Mike

Jana

CHAPTER 23

"Madeline, I don't disagree with you," said Michelle. "It's nice to have a man around, but I'm not convinced that part of the bargain, when I got married, was to be his mother. Nowhere in the wedding vows did it say I had to mother him. The minister didn't say love, honor and mother. It's one thing to have to do it for three children, that I can accept gladly, but not him too."

"Oh yes, I understand exactly what you are talking about," I said. "If it were my only job I might feel differently, but I also work full time. I guess being a male is their ticket to eternal childhood. Fortunately, not all men want to be mothered, and not all women want to mother. I don't mind when I'm not rushed to have to pick up after him. I just don't want to be expected to be the one always to do it or always to be in charge of making sure it's taken care of. I don't want to have to teach him to do simple household chores—a little cooking, some cleaning, how to use the washing machine and dryer. Just a little common courtesy, that's all I ask for."

"Maybe that's the problem, Jen. He thinks that women always do that stuff and it's a waste of his time to do it."

"Not in all cases. I know that my ex-husband's problem was his mother and father," said Deborah. "We were over there for dinner one night. My mother-in-law was in the kitchen cleaning up and my sister-in-law wanted to go in and help; but my mother-in-law wouldn't let her. When she finally sat down and got comfortable, my father-in-law told her to get him a glass of water. He didn't ask her, he told her. I couldn't believe my ears. My sister-in-law looked at him and said, 'I don't believe you'd ask such a thing.' Mother just sat down and she looked at her dad and said, 'Can't you get up and get your own water?' He was infuriated.

But it was my mother-in-law's reaction that I couldn't believe. She looked rather angrily at her daughter and said, 'Mind your own business. If he wants me to get him a glass of water, then it's my pleasure to do it.' When we drove home that night, my husband and I talked about what had happened. He told me his mother always got his father a glass of water in the middle of the night when he was thirsty, because she said it brought her pleasure to do it. He told me that his father had always taught him that women needed to take care of men to be happy—that it was their mission in life. The thought turned my stomach, but who was I to tell her how to love her husband?"

Marsha spoke up quietly, reliving a memory of her own, "I wonder how many of us look at our own parents' marriage or our in-laws' and think to ourselves, 'That's never going to happen to me.' Isn't that really the gist of what you're talking about, Deborah? Afterall, that's what Carol's been doing all night."

Deborah nodded in agreement and said, "My husband told me three years ago that the doctors thought his mother was dying of cancer. His father was miserable. For the first time in his life, my husband saw his father cry. He told me that his father begged God to save her. He would even give up smoking if God let her live. It sounded like my son praying to God, saying he'd give up his baseball mitt if God would answer his prayers. He valued his smoking and her life equally. I didn't know how to take it. By the way, he still smokes. Afterall, children rarely keep their promises, once they get what they want. He never kept his promise to God and she's forgiven him for it."

I thought of Steve and my own three children and wondered what they would offer God to save my life. Knowing Steve and the boys, it would be the television. Knowing my daughter, it would be my credit cards. And how long would those promises last if I survived? It didn't matter to him that smoking was detrimental to everyone around him, especially his wife. His fear was now alleviated—the fear that she would be taken away from him and that was all that counted. So he had negotiated with God to give up the most important thing he had left, cigarettes. I just hope my life is worth more than a cigarette to my family.

I can't speak for the others, but I sat there turning over in my mind what I'd learned about Deborah and the others this evening. How could I think the way Deborah chose to live was wrong? Carol thought all of us were, in some way, living wrong lives. After all, I was here tonight to escape for a little while. I tried to escape my daily problems, my feeling of loneliness and being trapped. I couldn't escape my feeling that I existed only to serve my family. Maybe when Deborah looks at me, she's thinking how unhappy I must be.

YOUR HONOR MY CLIENT ONLY WANTS TO DIVORCE
THE WIFE PART OF HIS MARRIAGE. HE WOULD LIKE TO
KEEP THE MOTHER PART OF HIS SPOUSE.

CHAPTER 24

I decided to lighten things up a little. "Did you know that
the male species has a gene that forces him to be
dependent on remote controls for television?" I asked
sarcastically. "The mere possession of the remote control is
as powerful a drive as sex is to them. They seem to be born
knowing how to work the remote. It has to be genetic.
Maybe someday scientists will find out what mutation
caused it. I think that a baby boy, if given a breast to suck
or a remote to punch, will take the remote every time and
punch it to a sporting event. Then, during the commercial,
he'll probably start crying to be fed." Every woman in the
room laughed as if they all knew what I was talking about.

I seemed to have brought up a common experience. "When my youngest son had trouble sleeping as a baby and would cry all night, nothing I could do would stop him. My husband walked in one night and said, 'Can't you stop his crying?' I was so tired that I just got up, handed my son over to my husband and told him to do it. Then, I went back to bed. All of a sudden the crying stopped. I waited to see if it was only temporary. But no, the silence went on, real silence. So I got up to see what he'd done. There in the lounge chair were my husband and six month old son watching ESPN, you know the sports channel, and in the baby's little hand was the infamous remote control. It was like a baby rattle for him. I couldn't believe my eyes. My husband bought my son a junior size remote control of his very own. If it weren't so cute watching them changing channels, I would have thrown the TV out. I think one day boys will be born with a remote control attached to their body. Evolution you know. Darwin didn't even figure on this one."

"I think television sports," said Madeline, "were invented to keep men away from women. Men have always had a fear of giving up their independence, so television became their savior. Men no longer even have to pretend to pay any attention to their wives. If you ever really want to punish your husband, just get the remote control before he does and watch him squirm all night. Then give it back to him and watch the look on his face. It's quite an expression. Almost looks orgasmic."

"The game," said Dottie, "at my retirement community, is the only activity that all the men get excited about. It's far more powerful than sex. You wouldn't believe how many of the ladies walked around, dying for male companionship. But all the men were interested in doing was watching sports, or talking about sports or dreaming about sports in their sleep. One night, an enterprising group of ladies decided to wear baseball uniforms to see if they could arouse the men. It almost worked. But out of frustration, I took the remote control from my husband and he followed me all the way to my bedroom. I decided to really test its power. I took it to the laundry room. It worked, he followed me without a thought. Then I went out and bought the most expensive deluxe remote control available and he's now in my control every night. It almost has the same power I had when I was a young lady holding out sexually. It would drive the men crazy. At my age I thank God for the invention of remote controls!"

Carol groaned, "Are you telling me that this is what I have to look forward to for the next fifty to sixty years?"

"Have you ever seen what a baby boy looks like in the womb?" I asked. "My obstetrician showed me a picture of the sonogram, I swear that little boy was sitting up with his hand out as if he were holding a remote control. He was practicing! I'm sure if you could see the baby boy in the womb when a ball game is on, he would be moving around or curled up in a completely different way than girls would. It's strictly genetic. It has to be."

"I wasn't joking when I asked that last question, you know," said Carol. "My boyfriend likes to watch TV, but I really like to talk—I need to talk. But he's not a talker. When we're at home together, he just wants to sit in front of the TV and maybe talk a little bit, but not like I do. I want to know what he did at work, who he met, who he talked to, what they said. It troubles me because, if he's like this now, what's he going to be like after we've been married for a few years? I tried to learn something about sports, so I could watch with him and have something to talk about, but he didn't have the patience to answer my questions."

"Carol? You can't get away from it," challenged Marsha. "I know things are beginning to change, but not enough yet. My husband and I have the same problem. I know exactly how you feel. I sit there and I feel as if he doesn't even know I exist. I hate it, because I want to talk to him. He gets this look of annoyance that only comes during television time. But when the commercial comes on, he turns off the sound, and, as if the mute button makes me appear like magic, he turns around to me and I become the sporting event, but only for a minute or two. It's my chance to ask questions, but I have to do it quickly because once the commercial's are over he puts the sound on again and I disappear."

"Even though my husband is an executive and prides himself on his communication skills, he has no clue on how to apply it to his personal life. He seems to have trouble looking at me for more than a few seconds at a time and I want his complete attention, like he gives the television. I think I'm as important as TV, but obviously he doesn't."

"I think God will have to make a female with a television built into her belly to have the perfect marriage of the future. That way men can't help but listen to us. I think my husband has bigger orgasms watching sports on his big screen TV than with sex. Sad, but true. I'm actually jealous of the TV because he doesn't finish with it and turn over and start snoring. Don't get me wrong. I like TV too. I just don't use it to get away from my spouse. Let's say I'm in the kitchen cooking and I'm trying to talk to him. He'll walk away as soon as he's had enough of me, right in the middle of a sentence. I'll say, 'come back here. I'm talking to you.' He'll yell from the family room, where the TV is on, 'I can hear you. I don't have to look you right in your eyes to know what you're saying, do I?'"

"But sometimes, when he's talking to me, I'll purposely walk away to give him a taste of his own medicine. He can't handle that. He wants that undivided attention too. He's like a child. If it doesn't affect him, he doesn't care. He doesn't understand that it bothers me when he walks away when I'm talking, as much as it bothers him when I walk away when he's talking to me. He sees no connection. He doesn't see how it discounts me. 'It's different,' he keeps repeating."

"When my husband," said Madeline, "walks into the house, the television always goes on. When he first pursued me, there was nothing more in his head than me. He couldn't wait to marry me; but then the TV became more attractive than me. Sometimes, I think he would have been happier married to the TV set. Sometimes I get really furious with him because we spend so little private time together. There he is, always glued to the damn TV set. To him, TV time is when we can cuddle up without really being together. He never realizes that I'm the one always cuddling up to him, not the other way around. Whenever I start talking, he shooses me until the commercial comes on. But now I have it down to a science. During the TV program, I get up and either cook, clean house or do the laundry; during the commercials we make love."

"Whew, every commercial?" asked Dottie, with a devilish look in her eyes.

"My husband?" Madeline laughed. "Do you even have to ask? Ha. But next week," she continued, "I'm cooking up a surprise for him. I'm making a tape of his favorite movie. I'll tell him it's running on one of the network channels and he won't know it's on tape. Then, after about twelve minutes of the movie, the first commercial will come on and we will begin making love. What he won't know, is that I will have edited in continuous commercials for half an hour so we'll have enough time for not decent sex, but unreal sex. It'll be called 'Commercial sex'. Ha, ha, ha."

CHILDREN, MAKE SURE YOU PUT AWAY YOUR FATHER'S TOYS BEFORE HE COMES HOME.

CHAPTER 25

"Men love sex, sports and toys," said Michelle. "But to my husband, they can be interchangeable—and do I have to explain myself?"

"Maybe to them, they're all the same thing," Bonnie said, obviously knowing something very private about her own husband, but would never tell the group.

Michelle went on, "My ex-husband was a railroad train freak. Whenever I got sick, he would go to the railroad tracks and sit there waiting for a train to go by. Any excuse he could find not to be with me would do. He couldn't stand it when I was sick. His train set was his favorite toy to play with. Sometimes, I think he loved his trains more than he loved me, even during our good years. He started out with a little train set when I met him and somehow, he got rolling on this humongous set. I don't know how it got so out of hand. I guess I have to take some of the blame, because I not only let him, I encouraged him. I just couldn't disappoint him. We started with a 4' x 4' block of wood, that went half way around the room. I painted the streets on for him. I even made little houses and later glued little people on the streets."

"When I finished making it, he wanted to have another power supply, so that he could run two trains in two directions. Because he had finished the new power supply, he then had to have a new set of tracks and more cars, so he tore the other one up and bought a much bigger block of wood. He couldn't decide where the tracks would go on it, so I had to decide for him."

"This was supposed to be his hobby, but he needed me to put it all together so he could play. I drafted it all up for him after he gave me a rough sketch of what he wanted. While he was at work, I drafted it to scale to make it right, because the way he had sketched it, would never have worked. I laid all the tracks down where they should go, since he couldn't follow the instructions on the paper that he had originally drawn up. Then he needed some switches to run it, so I designed a control box that was 2' x 3'. I put in all the switches, did all the wiring and hooked the whole thing up to the train. How much of this had he done? Nothing. He watched me do everything, like a child would do, while waiting impatiently for me to finish. Finally, he did do something. He went out and bought the trains that went on the tracks that I built. At first it lived in the middle of our unfurnished living room. Then I reached the point where I said, 'No more!' So I decided to move it to the closet in our bedroom. When I was seven and a half months pregnant, I moved this train set, as big as a queen-sized bed, standing four feet off the ground with two foot high mountains nailed on it. It had to fit into a closet and still be in operating condition. It was the best place for it to be stored that I could think of, but it drove me crazy to watch him shoving the clothes to one end and dragging the train out of the other end. He pulled half the clothes off their hangers every time he took the trains out to play with. Okay, so now that everything was completed, if I ever came into the room and interrupted his playing, he'd rudely ask me to leave, like a ten year old boy would ask his younger sister to get out of his treehouse. The nerve of him! It cracked me up that he showed off this train system that he supposedly built by himself to all his friends. You'll never believe what happened next, and my girlfriends will never forgive me for it—all of their husbands wanted one too. I wonder how many other wives got stuck building a toy like this for their husbands?"

"I'm married to a big, strong man," I said. "He's the same guy who grabs me like I'm a pipe wrench, but in reality, he's a big sweet pussycat, that just doesn't know his own strength. Well, this same man has a great attachment to his pillow. It's an old down pillow, about a quarter inch high by now. He will not part with that pillow, not even to let me get it restuffed. I've tried to get him to buy a new one, but he's had it since junior high school and won't get rid of it.

Actually, it's not even a pillow any more. It's a flat, workout piece of material with very little stuffing left. Whatever it is, it's disintegrated. He takes this pillow every night, fluffs it all up and says, 'Ooooh, it's starting to look like a pillow.' Then he takes his hand and hollows out one little section for his head. Then he lays his big head on his so-called pillow, but he's really laying it on the mattress because there's only a shadow of a pillow left. It's a good comfort for him to know his pillow is there, though."

"My fiance's favorite object is me," said Carol.

A couple of the ladies said in unison, "Oh, how cute!" Then they all cracked up laughing—even Deborah. "You know, it got to the point where I was beginning to think that a woman to him was 80% boobs, 19% crotch and 1% whatever else he wanted because that's all he seemed to know how to touch and play with. It was as if nothing else existed to him. I mean, he didn't even accidentally touch my shoulders or my head, not even accidentally, anymore."

"That's not so bad," said Bonnie. "My husband still plays in the bath. I can hear him in the tub with his little basketball and basket that attaches to the tile above the tub. Then he starts playing this weird game, 'I'm lord of the sky.' He says in a very deep voice, 'The rain god and the cloud gatherer who wields the awful thunderbolt—his power is greater than that of all the other divinities together.' He was actually playing Mythological God."

"Like a child, my husband doesn't think things out to their logical conclusion—like these rabbits he bought," said

Madeline. "Rabbits," laughed Michelle. "How old is your husband?" Madeline ignored Michelle's question. "He didn't think, that sure it'll be fun to wake up on Easter Sunday and have real live Easter bunnies, but come Monday morning, nobody would want to take care of them. That's why you buy chocolate rabbits, you eat them and then they're gone. But he didn't ask himself the logical question, 'What do you do with them after Easter?' About a month after he bought them though, he decided to cook them."

"No way," pleaded Carol. "He wasn't really going to eat those cute things, was he?"

"Actually Carol, they might have looked cute, but they were mean little rodents. So I gave them away because I wouldn't let my husband cook them. Besides, they weren't big enough to make anything more than soup. They also stunk up the house. I knew I'd have to take care of them after the holidays anyway. Another example is how he didn't consider the consequences of having a ninety pound dog. It never dawned on him what kind of mounds the dog was going to leave everywhere. Then of course, he refused to pick the mounds up and he didn't want to mow the lawn because of the dried dog mounds scattered over it. His excuse was he couldn't find a scooper big enough. So why bother. He just didn't think things through. I think he thought about as far ahead as my eight year old. He would think of all the fun things, not the responsible parts of anything." A silence fell over the group as we contemplated the various pets whose care and feeding we'd also been stuck with over the years.

WHEW! AM I GLAD 'GOD' GAVE WOMEN SPECIAL GENES TO DO THIS NATURALLY.

CHAPTER 26

"Going on vacation with a man is a real trip," said Madeline, "if you'll pardon the pun. When we go on vacation, we get to our destination and unpack. He wouldn't have any clothes to wear if I hadn't packed for him. He doesn't even ask me if I took anything for him. He just takes it for granted that I packed everything he'll need. In fact, the other day we went on a three day trip and we had to drop our dog off at a friend's house. About halfway there I said, 'Oh God, I forgot the dog food,' and he looked at me like, 'Oh, that's really great.' And I thought, 'I don't believe this! Here I am remembering it and he assumed that I was responsible for it all along.' Like, what made me responsible? It's his dog as much as mine. Give me a break."

"Speaking of vacations," said Marsha, looking as if Madeline's situation was nothing compared to hers, "my husband doesn't even know what packing is except that, somehow the clothes make it into the luggage, and when we get home it gets back in his drawers and onto his hangers."

"God, my husband is a book all by himself," I said. "When we go on vacation and we pack, all I can say is packing is no big deal—I do all the packing. There really isn't anything to discuss. I do it all, period. I plan the clothes for all of us. I set out little outfits for all of them. These pants will go with this shirt and this shirt; this shirt will go with these pants this many times and you can wear these socks with it; and you need at least two extra pair of underwear in case somebody has an accident. Every time he goes on a business trip, let's say for three days, I pack five pairs of underwear. I'll pack extras of everything and write directions for him, so he knows what goes with what."

"I think one of the biggest mistakes I made, and am still making as a woman and mother, is I'm always doing for my family, instead of teaching them to do without me," said Marsha. "And another thing that bothers me is, I don't think I expect the same things of my boys that I do of my daughter and I'm not sure how to change that expectation—or lack of expectation. I'm not even sure I want to. Wow! I can't believe I just said that. I wonder how many of you think the same way and are afraid to admit it?" A silence landed like a thud in the room. No one moved. Everyone looked in deep thought about their own lives. You know the way I am about silence, so I spoke up. "I don't want my daughter to turn out like a man, but I'd like to see her have some ambitions beyond domestic ones. And I don't want my boys to be effeminate, but I sure hope they turn out better husbands than their father—I mean, more communication, more helping around the house, more responsibility for themselves." I paused a moment, and thought to myself. "I also don't want a husband who does everything for me. I don't want him around the house like I am. He'd drive me nuts like retired men tend to do with their wives. I just want him to volunteer without me asking. That asking would also drive me nuts."

"I don't know about you ladies, but I could handle a wife like me," Madeline joked. "I actually like taking care of my family. I love doing things for them. I just don't want to be expected to do everything. I agree with you Jenny; I want him to volunteer to help, not wait to be asked. I want him to share. I think there's a difference between nurturing and mothering. I don't want to be his mother, but I love nurturing him. I would also love to be nurtured in return sometimes."

"I agree with a lot of what Marsha said, but I still feel confused," Bonnie said. "Most men still believe that the problems in relationships today are due to women having crossed the sex boundaries and therefore becoming more masculine. I guess nobody knows what to expect anymore of one another. You'll also notice who they place the responsibility for the problem on. So here's the problem, without expectations we don't know our place in a relationship, but it's when I'm expected to do everything that I resent him."

"Okay," said Carol changing the tone in the room. "I have

to admit this has been great, making fun of the men in our lives. I just have a couple of questions. Who's supposed to do the changing? What changes are we supposed to make? I'm happily engaged, if we change, will we still be happy? I mean, I don't want a shadow of myself. If we were completely alike, then what would we be as a couple? You know, I'm not even sure what I'm asking. Maybe all I want to know is, if I don't want him acting the way the typical man does, then how do I want him to act?"

"It's confusing to us too," said Marsha. "So can you imagine how the poor men feel, losing jobs and status to women? Now they are expected to express emotions they were taught they were not supposed to have. We have one hell of a mess. I feel a little different from you. I don't mind cooking. I don't mind cleaning. I love listening to all their problems and making things better. I don't like laundry, but I've trained my husband to help. I think I'd be lost if I stopped doing for everyone."

"I agree with you, Marsha," I said, feeling relieved that I wasn't the only one feeling confused. "I don't want to be expected to be the one who is responsible all the time. I just don't want to be relied on to do everything."

"Oh God!" yelled Michelle as she held up her wrist watch. "I don't want to be a party pooper ladies, but has anyone bothered to look at the time lately?" Simultaneously, we looked at our watches. It was nearly midnight. "Is anybody going to buy anything from me?" asked Marsha, hoping we'd all feel obligated. "Unfortunately, the party's over ladies. I have to go to work tomorrow, but please come up and look at what I have."

Michelle walked up to me and asked if I was going to buy anything. "Michelle, I'm going to have a tough enough time explaining this prize to Steve. He didn't know where I was going tonight, remember?"

"I'll tell you what, ladies," Marsha called out. "I'll sell everything at a 25% discount tonight." I was now tempted to see what she was selling. My husband always kidded me when I knew a sale was taking place. We spent about another half hour chatting, laughing, and trying on clothes. "Are you ready Jenny?" asked Michelle, as she put on her jacket. I said goodnight to the women and thanked Marsha. I bought some sexy panties that I thought Steve might like on me. Some of the things Marsha had, I just wasn't ready to buy yet, although they sure got me thinking. Dottie spent around five hundred dollars on everything she could carry. "Marsha, maybe next time you'll show me some of the real toys you have," I said nervously, meaning what I said. "Maybe I'll even buy some." "Yeah sure," laughed Michelle. "You'll see, Marsha. I'll call you, I promise."

As we were leaving, I looked back and saw Madeline and Dottie comparing the things they bought. Dottie was more than okay for someone her age. She was living life on the light side. That was more than I could have said about my own life, before tonight.

Michelle and I walked outside and got into her car without saying a word. As we drove away, she finally asked me, "Well, was it worth it?"

"Yeah, I have to admit it was fun. It was nice hearing that other women have the same complaints I do. I don't feel alone any more. It's funny, I don't even feel tired and usually by this time I've fallen in bed exhausted and would have been asleep for a couple of hours by now."

"I don't know if that's good," joked Michelle as we drove around the corner. "It doesn't say much for us, does it?"

"Maybe, maybe not. Maybe I can laugh at myself a little now, instead of being so serious and tired all the time. Maybe, I learned I just don't 'have to' anymore."

"Have to what?" she asked me curiously.

"Have to anything. Before tonight, I believed everything was my responsibility. I had to make sure that it was going to get done, whatever 'it' was, because if I didn't, who would?"

"And now?" "I'm not sure yet, but I think I just don't have to. Nothing is that important to run myself ragged for everyone else if it destroys me in the process, just because nobody else will do it. As I said, I just don't 'have to.' That's all."

LIFE IN THE 'TOOS'.

CHAPTER 27

The drive home from the party was fun. Michelle and I just joked about silly things, the way we had when we were in high school together. I hadn't done that for too many years. I had forgotten how to just let go. Being a mom had made me too serious about life. Taking on everyone's problems has made me think too much about everybody else. I worried about everything, except how to just let go and have fun. I had turned into wife and mother to the point where I'd lost Jennifer somewhere along the way. Tonight, I didn't spend all my time worrying about everyone being okay, so that I'd feel okay. I felt more okay than I had in a long time.

We drove the last few minutes in a companionable silence. When Michelle pulled up to my house, I turned to her and said, "Thanks Michelle, I'm really grateful for tonight and I want to go out more." I felt very peaceful. "One night a week, maybe? Okay?" She reached over and squeezed my hand. "Sure," she smiled as I got out.

For a moment I paused and stood looking at my home. I felt a little apprehensive about going back in and returning to my old life. It seemed as if I'd been gone for weeks, not hours. There had been too many days in my life recently, when I thought of disappearing for awhile—maybe a long while—and just living with me, thinking about me, concentrating on me, pampering me and mothering me. As a matter of fact, I'm going to start a new business. I'm going to go into the catering business. I'm going to cater a real delicacy—ME—all of me, every whim and every desire. As a matter of fact, if anyone wants to go in the catering business with me, I'll be more than happy to let you cater to me too.

I looked around, slowly savoring the familiar scene, the neighborhood rooftops and the trees along the street. A melancholy silence drifted through the hills. The evening dew had long since set in. The lights from my house sparkled on the dewy lawn, that seemed to reflect the stars above the canyon. All the normal, neighborhood, daytime sounds were absent.

I opened the front door, turned to wave goodbye to Michelle and quietly stepped through the doorway into another world. I returned to a world that was my previously expected identity and reality. Suddenly, I realized I was still holding my ridiculous prize from the party. I wondered if Steve would be amused or even notice it.

I tiptoed through the house. Not because I was trying not to wake anyone, actually I was trying to avoid being heard because, I didn't want to talk to Steve, the kids or even Stanley the dog for that matter. I wanted to savor the evening for just awhile longer.

Tonight, I found out that maturity isn't a virtue. For that matter, it's not very much fun either. I forgot how to do the fun things I did when I first met Steve. Who made the rule that we had to stop doing the silly, frivolous things we did when we were young. Those were the things that made us fall in love. It's funny, if we did it all in reverse, if we were too mature, too responsible, too mechanical and all the rest of the things we become as mature adults working so hard to take care of the everyday things we place so much importance on, probably not too many people would ever fall in love. So why do we do it? I guess, because we're taught that's the way grown ups are supposed to be. Well I'm here to tell you, we are all born with a male and female side; we're also born with an adult and a child side. And I intend on spending more time with the child in me.

I think the secret of happiness comes down to understanding one word. It's a very important word to really pay attention to. That word is "TOO". Whenever you do anything with the word "TOO" in it, watch out! We get caught up in the "TOO" muchs, "TOO" hards, "TOO" difficults, "TOO" much efforts, "TOO" lates, "TOO" expensives, "TOO" cheaps, "TOO" much like thems, "TOO" many bills, "TOO" hard to try, "TOO" tired, "TOO" little love, "TOO" much work, just too many "TOO's" to ever be happy. Well, I took my life "TOO" seriously for "TOO" long. I did "TOO" much of everything for "TOO" many people and "TOO" little for me. I have a friend that once told me, "To be happy and always grow, I should never be afraid to make mistakes, because with mistakes you create the miracle of growth. To grow you must use the Goldilocks syndrome, you must do things "TOO" much one way, then "TOO" much the other way to ever find your HAPPY medium." Life is "TOO" special to take anything "TOO" seriously or "TOO" anything for that matter.

I quietly looked around the house and took a very slow and deep breath. I couldn't help hearing that the television was still on, turned down low, but the rest of the house was dark, silent, peaceful and all mine for the moment.

Heh! A perfect ending to a new beginning.

THE END
(But there's more)

AFTERWARD

This book is based on the perceptions of the women interviewed. It's not designed to bash men or women, but to express the frustrations and perceptions that exist in their everyday world.

Truth is not reality, perception is. Until we listen, really listen and respect one another's "perceptions", especially when they're different than our own, we can never achieve happy and successful relationships. Eventually, someone feels discounted. So often, when we meet someone new that we think has the same beliefs and perceptions as we do, we get very excited. When we later find out their perceptions really weren't the same, our relationship begins to deteriorate.

We really can't hear what others say until we're willing to respect the other person's perceptions; we'll always place ourselves in a position of being right and them as wrong. We're so interested in getting our point across that we have an answer to what they're saying before they even finish. This always results in disappointment and in the placing of one's own expectations over their perception. How can we really hear if we don't trust and respect where other people are coming from. We're so busy trying to prove we're right, we forget why we liked them in the first place.

Too many of us expect others to do, and be something, because we are a certain way or because we are told and expected to be a particular way. It never worked before and never will work in the future. But trusting in the difference of the perceptions of others helps us truly see and hear those in our lives and will bring about greater happiness.

However, if only one person does the understanding, it may be worse than no one taking the time to listen. If one person is always understanding and the other person feels they're always right, the understanding person is always discounted. That's one of the reasons this book was written. It's so easy to be taken advantage of, if balance is not achieved right from the start. Did you ever notice that when a relationship is out of balance and the person that is always understanding and doing for the person or persons that are being done for, when things go wrong, it's always the fault of the understanding person. They're always trying to live up to everyone else's expectations and always fall short. In the beginning of the relationship, the understanding person feels needed and the partner that is always taken care of feels great. They finally met someone that understands them and wants to do for them and even thinks like them. Trouble! Both people are expected to act a certain way and both expect the other to stay that way forever. By the way, that's another part of the problem. I believe expectations are the most debilitating social disease known to mankind, they've caused wars, physical and emotional abuse, loss of lives, divorce, breakdown of families and the list goes on. Yet without expectations we can't grow, business can't succeed, high levels of achievement can't be attained. It's like eating, if you eat to fuel the body efficiently, the body will work smoothly. If you fuel it excessively with junk, it will breakdown, but if you don't fuel it at all, you'll die. I guess it comes down to the word "TOO" again. Don't live your life in the "TOO"s', stay balanced! Take the time to listen to the perception of those around you, but never discount your own because you think you're supposed to be a certain way. You're THAT important. Remember that! You're THAT important!

I want to thank all the people who have shared their lives with me. You've made a major difference in mine. Yet, I haven't told a fraction of the stories yet to be told. I would love to hear from you, my publisher would love to hear from you, because who knows what stories will be told in future books.